SAVE A DECADE!

SAVE A DECADE!

HOW TO WORK EFFECTIVELY, STARTING NOW!

PAUL DUDUIT

SAVE A DECADE!
HOW TO WORK EFFECTIVELY, STARTING NOW!

iUniverse books may be ordered through booksellers or by contacting:

iUniverse
1663 Liberty Drive
Bloomington, IN 47403
www.iuniverse.com
1-800-Authors (1-800-288-4677)

Because of the dynamic nature of the Internet, any web addresses or links contained in this book may have changed since publication and may no longer be valid. The views expressed in this work are solely those of the author and do not necessarily reflect the views of the publisher, and the publisher hereby disclaims any responsibility for them.

Any people depicted in stock imagery provided by Getty Images are models, and such images are being used for illustrative purposes only. Certain stock imagery © Getty Images.

ISBN: 978-1-5320-6259-9 (sc)
ISBN: 978-1-5320-6260-5 (e)

Library of Congress Control Number: 2018913517

Print information available on the last page.

iUniverse rev. date: 11/12/2018

CONTENTS

DEDICATION

There are many people who have had a great influence on my life and I apologize to those I inadvertently don't mention. Without question, my greatest influencer and head cheerleader is my wife of 51 years, Mary Patricia, who was without fail a positive, happy, cheerful, encouraging voice of comfort on the other end of the phone when I called her from wherever I was in the world, as I spent most of my career traveling. She still lovingly fills that role and is the best Christian I have ever known. As I am allergic to Microsoft Word, I owe a special thank you to Alice and Fred Zeigler who made my final draft look presentable.

I

INTRODUCTION

When I first started working with computers, I used to keep a 2X4 leaning against the wall of my office to wake up my computer, get its attention, and get it to do what I wanted it to do.

Now that I have captured your attention, interest, and imagination, here are 5 reasons why you should read and practice what I tell you in this book:

1. *Desire* – you should want to Save a Decade (10 years) of your working life by believing what I tell you in this book about *getting experience now*, and avoid the slow learning process of the past.
2. *Value* – you should want to receive the highest reward, however you measure it, for the remainder of your working life.
3. *Audience* – anyone, regardless of age, gender, or profession can add the principles in this book to their current skill set.

4. *Basis* – I've seen a lot of good and bad work practices and worked in several industries in 54 countries, so have some faith and trust that I know what I'm talking about in this book.

5. *Gender Neutral* – I had to write this book from a male perspective, but if you can find a masculine pronoun in this book, other than in the context of an anecdote, I'll send you a free copy of this book.

II

WHAT IS THE PURPOSE OF THIS BOOK?

I have wanted to write this book for a long time because I've always been fascinated by the successful and un-successful people I've observed and kept wondering why it was happening. When I was working, I spent a lot of time on airplanes (and I can't sleep on airplanes) and in hotel rooms, read a lot of books, and collected articles and scraps of paper that I thought would someday reach coherence. I scrawled an outline, wrote chapters, and generally made a mess of the whole thing, but I pronounced it progress. I realized that I didn't have a clue about what I was doing, but I just kept writing. When I stopped working, I continued with a yellow pad of paper, sitting in my recliner, with an occasional glass of an adult beverage, and this time I think I have made sense of the whole process. It took me a year to go through withdrawal from working, get over continuous jet lag, cancel my sleep debt, and begin a chapter at a time to create this book.

I have always thought that regardless of what level of education you achieve, almost everyone then gets a job, but then don't have a clue about how to go about working. School teaches you theory and then you have to figure out how to put all that learning into practice. I don't believe it matters what profession you choose, your gender, or your age, but everyone has to figure things out for themselves. My life was a giant Rubik's cube and I had to keep rearranging the pieces until I found something that worked for me. And nobody tells you about any of the secret codes and handshakes because all of them had to go through the same process! So you spend your first few years in a giant pinball machine, make lots of mistakes, make many false starts and stops, go down lots of rabbit trails, and mainly through trial and error (lots of errors), you slowly figure out what works best for you and how to become at least competent at whatever it is you are doing.

I have noticed that some professions, predominately populated in the past by women, do get training before going to work: teachers and nurses are obvious. Airline pilots are the only masculine profession that comes to mind, but all 3 of these professions are changing their approach to staffing.

I think the magic number is about 10 years, give or take, and it's different for every person, before the lights come on, you realize that you've seen this same problem before, and you know how to solve it. You've just been touched with the magic wand called *Experience*. It's also about the time that you've demonstrated to your bosses that you're not hopeless and can be trusted with more and more responsibilities. It's a process!

I've been playing a lot of duplicate bridge the last 4 years and the game mimics the workplace in so many ways. I treat every bridge hand like a puzzle: what information do I know, what don't I know, what are the strengths and weaknesses of my hand, what have the other 3 players at the table told me about their hands by their bidding and play of the hand, and how well did my partner and I play the hand. We're keeping score! Some players are better than others at counting the cards, remembering what has been played, considering the probabilities, and making rational decisions. It's a lot like a job!

Bob Hamman, arguably the best current bridge player in the US and winner of multiple national and world titles said that, "The good players play poorly and the rest play worse." He's not trying to be funny – the same type of analytic thinking should take place at the bridge table as well as in the workplace, but it doesn't !

I've worked in 54 countries and I've seen abysmal work practices everywhere, and I'm not excluding this country at all. What were they thinking? Oh, that's right, they weren't.

But what if you didn't have to wait about 10 years to work effectively starting right now? What if I could tell you how you could be doing your job better right now, and I don't care what your job is, or your gender, or your age, or your education level? *That is the intent of this book.*

I could sum up this book in one word, the famous old motto that sits on the desk of every person who works at IBM: *THINK!* But then that would be a very short book and I wouldn't get the thrill of telling you all the cool stuff I've learned. But so many people don't think. They seem to have left their brains at home or in the trunks of their cars. What a mental image! It's just mental laziness.

This book is gender neutral. The world is not. Women are the most under-utilized portion of the workforce. Let's start changing that!

It was difficult to write this book without using masculine pronouns. Try it sometime. It's harder than you think, if you're male.

III

WHO SHOULD READ THIS BOOK?

Anyone can use this book, regardless of where you are in your life cycle!

Please remember the purpose of the book: jump start your career by more quickly gaining *experience* instead of the lengthy painful approach of the past. You should want to seek more efficient and effective methods of working instead of feeling like you're in the great pinball machine of life. Be proactive in how you think about and perform your job, regardless of the field of endeavor you pursue, instead of just being reactive. Reflective is another good word to add to your vocabulary.

Anyone can picture the examples I talk about and can visualize situations and people that they have had to deal with so far in their careers. You can probably add chapter topics of your own. Go for it ! Send me copies.

IV

WHY SHOULD YOU LISTEN TO ME? IT'S MY FIRST BOOK!

I've spent a lifetime watching people and it's been a fascinating parade. I've had lots of different paying jobs in lots of different industries since I moved on from mowing lawns. Let me also say right away that I didn't plan any of my career – it just happened ! I've now lived in the same house in Dallas for 40 years and had 9 different jobs in the first 36 years here in Dallas. One job just seemed to follow after the last job and I just kept showing up. I laugh at people who talk about planning their careers or their lives. Good luck with that ! John Lennon said that life is what happens when you're making other plans. The best you can do is try to make good decisions when seeking your next job.

None of this is intended as bragging – I've just done a lot of fun and interesting stuff. Please see Appendix A for the gory details.

My most interesting learning experiences with people:

- Funeral home – learned to play gin rummy in back of a hearse; people's emotions come out at funerals; broke up fistfights; changed flat tires during funerals; broke into locked churches
- Bartender – remembering orders and working for tips; it's all about taking care of and paying attention to the customer
- Steel mill – first experience with shift work and working in a union operation
- Liquor store chain – my only direct contact with working in the retail world; a very interesting business
- US & world travel – dynamite experience; never had a problem anywhere; saw every place except India; met nice people everywhere I went.

A friend of mine said that every job he has had was a temporary job – some just lasted longer than others did.

Jerry Garcia of the Grateful Dead said, "What a long, strange trip it's been." Amen, brother.

V

MORALS & ETHICS

I put this chapter at the front of the book because if you don't have morals and practice ethics, you're dead before you even start working. This is not a philosophical or religious statement. If you lie, cheat, or steal, no one will want to work with you, customers and clients will desert you, and no one will ever trust you. If you don't have morals and ethics, either get some, or *stop reading this book right now*. You'll just be wasting your time.

I think morals are simply what you believe to be right versus wrong. "Thou shalt not steal" sounds the same whether expressed by Protestantism, Judaism, Catholicism, or Islam. When confronted with a situation, how do you think, or how do you feel? Those are morals. They should be engrained.

Your morals come from: parents, teachers, family, friends, religious training, and examples you see in other people.

I think of ethics as how you act (or react) when confronted with a situation or a choice. Ethics are what you do or what you practice.

Is the glass half full, half empty, twice as big as it needs to be, or big enough to hold my teeth? There are no wrong answers here, but ethical questions are rarely this easy.

EXAMPLE 1: When I moved to the New York City headquarters office of my first employer after college, I was required to attend the company ethics course – some lecture on company policies, some illustrative examples, some elementary business law principles, lots of discussion, and then a quiz. I think the purpose of the course was for everyone to hear the same thing at the same time and for everyone to hear how the company expected us to behave in our interactions with customers, suppliers, and within our own company with each other. I'm not bragging but I finished the quiz fairly early and looked around the room to see that everyone else was still working. The erasers were flying, clouds of eraser crumbs in the air – yikes, I had better go back over what I had done. When the seminar leader began reviewing the quiz with all of us, it seemed to me that a lot of the people in the room (no, I'm not going to put a number on it) were not trying to decide on the *right* course of action, they were trying to figure out what they could get away with. I was also struck by how different everyone was: schools, college degrees, race, work experience, geography, gender, military training, and religion – kind of like America.

I was a white, male, chemical engineer from rural Ohio, with no military background, and an abundance of religious training. My mother drug her 5 kids to church every Sunday morning, Sunday night, and Wednesday night prayer meeting (to get us through to the next Sunday). I had the rules of "Right and Wrong" drilled into me for 17 years. If a tent meeting was being held (it was literally a big tent in an open field, chairs on the grass, lights, P/A system, no A/C, and all the mosquitoes, chiggers, and fleas you could swat away with the fans supplied by the local funeral home. We were there every night. Attendance was not optional and neither was good behavior.

The company's seminar leader was trying to rein everyone in and get us on the same page in the songbook, sort of like herding cats. The discussions were the most interesting part of the seminar to me, as I was trying to understand how everyone was thinking and how they arrived at their conclusions - how their minds were working.

EXAMPLE 2: *City of Dallas.* Once upon a time, just a few years ago, there was a guy who ran a family-owned business that he had inherited from his father and grandfather. The company did small construction jobs, street repairs, storm sewer repairs, and water line repairs. But he couldn't get work for his company from the City of Dallas. He knew that other companies like his were getting work. His company employed his kids, his siblings, his in-laws, cousins, and family friends and they would all be out of work if he couldn't find some more jobs for his company. He found out that he needed to pay *commissions* or make *donations* to political campaigns if he wanted to get jobs for his company, so he finally gave in and did that, and got caught up in a corruption scandal. He took a plea deal and spent 16 months in jail. The assistant mayor of Dallas got a 20 year jail sentence. The company went broke and everyone was out of work. He knew what the *right* choice was. He made a decision and suffered the consequences, along with his entire family. What choice would you have made with all of those people being dependent on you?

EXAMPLE 3: Lance Armstrong was the best cyclist in the world, on a level playing field, but the field wasn't level. His competitors were drugged up, storing blood transfusions, and flaunting rules officials whose laxness would have been a kind description. Everybody else was cheating and getting away with it and he wasn't competitive. What would you do? By the way, Lance's sponsors were paying him big bucks to parade their logos in front of the world as part of a winning team, and he couldn't win. What would you do? He knew what was *right* and what was *wrong*. He made a choice and he paid the price.

EXAMPLE 4: A key interest rate usually known as the London Interbank Offered Rate, referred to as *LIBOR*, may be simply defined as the lowest rate at which a bank in London would loan money to another bank before the doors open for business that day, kind of a benchmark or indicator of the financial health of the country's banking system. LIBOR is the basis upon which all other interest rates and exchange rates in the financial markets are calculated. It is a very complex topic which I am simplifying here to make a point. The mechanism is that a committee asks 18 banks for their quotes, throws out the 4 highest quotes, throws out the 4 lowest quotes, and averages the remaining 10 quotes. Sounds reasonable, right? *All 18 banks lied.* A major scandal blew up in 2012, 9 figure fines to several banks, many resignations, many firings, and of course Parliament passed more laws. The bankers had quickly figured out that if they fudged the LIBOR quotes just a tad bit higher, they would make more money in all of their lines of business, as they were defining the basis. Just a 0.01% change in LIBOR was worth several million dollars to each bank. The temptation was too great.

Mike Tyson (this may be the first time he's ever been quoted in a book) said that, "Everybody's got a plan, until someone hits you in the mouth." How will you react when life hits you in the mouth? How will you act or react when confronted with a situation you didn't expect or had never envisioned?

It's very easy to sit on your white throne of purity, cloaked in your legal clothing, and pass judgment on others, unless and until you're in their shoes, and face some tough choices.

It's not so easy, at times, to look at yourself in the mirror every day and know that you made the right decision, regardless of the costs.

Lewis Grizzard quote: "Don't judge. It's not your job. God's got that."

Don't lie – it's so easy and so tempting. But you will usually end up telling another lie to bolster the first lie, et cetera, ad nauseum. It will *always* catch up with you.

But then Mark Twain spoke up and said, "Always tell the truth. That way, you never have to remember what you said. But on the other hand, anybody can keep track of a few lies." I'm sure he was kidding, I think.

Don't lie to or cheat your clients and customers. They will find out and your company will lose multiples of the business in the future that you tried to get dishonestly, forever. Clients and customers are like elephants – they never forget anything. They will get even, and they're mean SOBs when crossed.

It's easy to brand the Latin American drug suppliers as criminals and become very righteous about stopping them, arresting them, throwing them in jail, or throwing them out of our country. It's a popular narrative. But stop and think about who is buying the drugs? I'm not denying that many of them are the suppliers. But where is the demand coming from? Now tell me who are the bad guys?

Question: How will you know if you have morals and ethics?

Answer: You do the right thing, even when no one is watching. *Right* is defined within you.

VI

UNDERSTANDING OUR WORLD

a. LEARNING FROM HISTORY

Everyone in our country needs to understand how we got to where we are. All businesses must assess the geographical backdrop to their decisions and sometimes don't. You need to understand the answers to the following questions. If you don't know the answers, look them up:

o   Why are all major cities in the world located on water?
o   How did the US start on the upper East Coast and grow to the west?
o   How and why did the Post Office develop?
o   How important is safe drinking water?
o   Why were human beings given 2 opposable thumbs?
o   Why was the interstate highway system built?
o   Why did telegraphs rise and fall as a business (it's the 2nd T in AT&T)?
o   How many times did Thomas Edison try and fail to invent an electric light bulb?

- Why did George Westinghouse and Edison fight over AC versus DC?
- Why do our 2 political parties even exist, other than as a way to divvy up power?
- How many times did Henry Ford go bankrupt before perfecting the assembly line for cars?
- Why did cars come with buggy whip holders?
- Why is it still called a glove compartment?
- How did John D. Rockefeller get so rich?
- Why did Ross Perot become wealthy selling software from the trunk of his car?
- How did Richard Branson start his airline?
- How did Bill Gates go from college dropout to building Microsoft?
- How did Steve Jobs envision iPads and iPhones when he was building MACs?
- Is the internet the most revolutionary phenomenon to ever hit the world?
- Would solar power and wind power even exist and continue to grow without tax credits? Is that a wise use of our tax dollars for established technology?
- How fast are retail stores failing?
- Why is our jury system such a poor method of meting out justice?
- Did you know that Google is a number, 1 followed by 100 zeroes? Actually, that's a mis-spelling. The correct word is Googul. Doesn't look as spiffy as Google.
- Who ever thought nuclear power would be green?
- How has banking changed?
- How fast will the need for more office buildings, roads, and transportation decrease as more people work from home?

o   How fast can our government and legal system adjust to the exponential changes in the electronic world where business now exists?

o   If Max Steinke had discovered water in 1937 (as the king of Saudi Arabia had hired him to do) instead of oil, how would the world be different?

o   Is California determined to freeze to death thirsty, in the dark, on foot?

b. HOW DOES THE WORLD WORK?

Fortunately, we have a great teacher. His name is Henry Kissinger, you may have heard of him. His recent book called **World Order** (Touchstone, 2014) explains through history, warfare, trade, religion, and economics how we have arrived where we are. It's probably the most interesting book I have ever read. Regardless of your political persuasion, *Read This Book*. It is not a dry, academic tome and it explains in easy to understand language how the world got to where it is today.

Henry Kissinger was born in Germany and immigrated to the US at age 15. He went to high school and college here, was drafted into the Army in World War II, and served as a rifleman in Germany, oddly enough. He earned a PHD in government with a 383 page thesis that forever limited the size of future theses at Harvard. He has been a tenured professor, government adviser in several administrations, National Security Adviser and Secretary of State under President Nixon, and was awarded the Nobel Peace Prize in 1973 for his efforts in ending the Vietnam War.

He asks us to imagine 5 large organisms covering the surface of the earth with their influences, slowly changing and rubbing up against each other and/or butting heads. They expand, contract, cause friction, invade, gain territory, lose territory, fight wars with each other, trade with each other, move people around, etc. It is a fascinating read, and he explains it so logically and eloquently without your having to consult a dictionary to understand what he is saying.

- USA
- Europe
- Russia
- China
- Islam

He ignores the other parts of the world because they are economically much smaller. His carving of the world map tells the story of these 5 regions through their history and evolution to their current form.

What is fascinating to me is that these 5 groups define our current world and their interactions define our world's economy and world peace/war.

It is highly recommended, clear, and easy to read because everyone in the business world needs to understand how all the pieces mesh, especially when someone throws sand in the gearbox. Regardless of your occupation, you need to understand how the world works and learn to ignore the 24/7 drivel masquerading as *news* that litters print media, television, and the internet. *They* have to fill up all that air time and sell all that advertising. Please accept that we only know what *they* want us to know. The *news* is managed every hour of every day.

We may not want to know or need to know everything that's going on in the world. Keep your salt shaker handy !

Kissinger does a masterful job of cutting through all the dross and telling a coherent story.

c. BILL MOYERS AND THE GROUP OF 100

As a veteran TV newsman, political commentator, and a proud graduate of the University of Texas, he was invited to give the commencement address in Austin, TX in 2000. Instead of platitudes, Mom, and apple pie, his talk was short and just a bunch of statistics, none of which have changed significantly in the ensuing years. He asked the new graduates to think of the world in percentages, that is a group of 100 people that represented the entire world's population, and think about the implications and messages they could derive from examining these numbers. They are very sobering and thought provoking, especially when viewed from a cloistered, privileged perch in our country:

- o 57 Asian
- o 21 European
- o 14 North & South American
- o 8 African
- o 52 female, 48 male
- o 30 are white, 70 are of color
- o 80 live in sub-standard housing
- o 50 are malnourished
- o 1 has a college education
- o 1 has a computer

Just six people (not part of the above group of 100 people) in the entire world control 59% of the world's wealth, and all six are in the USA.

Bust out of the tiny, tiny bubble in which you live and work ! Where do you fit in the above statistics? What do the above statistics tell you about your profession or the company in which you are working?

d. THEORY VS PRACTICE

I'm personally not that interested in theory except how to apply it, how to use it, how to put it into practice, how to do something with it. Accounting and Finance can tell you where the problems are – numbers are indicators that alert you to dangers/opportunities – numbers might be interesting by themselves but it's what you do with them that's important. Moses sent 12 spies into the Promised Land and the vote was 10-2 not to send the children of Israel in. The majority is not always right, they're just the majority. It's a convenient way to make decisions that may ignore discussion or thinking. Voting may be the only practical avenue when large numbers of people are involved. Benevolent dictators sound like great answers and may be wonderful, but they're hard to find. When the failure to solve a problem is too horrible to contemplate, then drastic, seemingly unthinkable answers become absolutely necessary – see Dirty Harry movies and books by Vince Flynn. It's idealistic to think the *bad guys* will play by the *rules* but we see an endless number of examples of them defying order.

VII

WHY YOU MUST UNDERSTAND YOUR OWN SELF

a. IT'S YOU AGAINST THE WORLD

Now, what are you going to do?

At a minimum, you need food, clothing and shelter.

Heat would be nice when it's cold – air conditioning would be nice when it gets warm.

Are you going to walk everywhere?

Let's assume you can't depend on parents, family, or friends.

You need to earn money ! What can you do?

What salable skills can you offer to an employer?

Do you see that your life's focus has shrunk to a desperate need for cash, at the speed of light?

You may now realize that you need additional salable skills.

How do you pay for more education? You could work and save some money.

You are a product of the environment in which you have grown up, to now.

There are no do-overs in life. It's a brutal fact you must accept very early.

You can only keep going from where you are, starting now. Norton Cuban, the father of three sons including Mark Cuban (billionaire owner of the Dallas Mavericks) told his sons that you will never be any younger than you are today, so don't waste time. You're burning daylight.

Nobody ever won a game they didn't play.

You will always miss 100% of the shots you don't take.

Don't be a bystander.

The world is *not* waiting for you to make the first move.

Buddha: "No one saves us but ourselves. No one can and no one may. We ourselves must walk the path."

How do you define success? *Leonard Cohen*: "Success is survival."

b. WHO ARE YOU?

The song was recorded in 1978 by the rock group *The Who*, written by Pete Townshend with lyrics and performance by Roger Daltrey.

The song may be best known as the theme music for the original *CSI* television series which was set in Las Vegas. The words of the song describe what the forensic scientists were trying to figure out every week on the show. The chief forensics investigator was Gil Grissom and Dr. Al Robbins always seemed to be performing those gruesome autopsies while we were trying to eat dinner.

As you pursue your career, this is the most relevant question you can answer when you look in the mirror in the morning and as you work away at your job.

Please understand that there are no wrong answers, but everyone needs to take an inventory (and write down their own answers). Imagine that you are trying to get your arms around what may seem to be a nebulous, slippery, ever-changing personality, *You*:

- o   What are your strengths?
- o   What types of tasks do you do well?
- o   What are your weaknesses?
- o   Do you despise staring at a computer screen all day? Or do you love it?
- o   Are you comfortable interacting with co-workers?
- o   Are you comfortable working alone?
- o   Are you comfortable interacting with strangers?
- o   Do you enjoy finding problems?

o   Do you enjoy solving problems?
o   Are you content with completing routine tasks?
o   Do you like working with a team to solve complex problems?
o   Do you take pride in your work?
o   Do you watch the clock all day long?
o   Do you like taking on responsibility?
o   Do you think you are an introvert or an extrovert at heart?
o   Do you feel like you fall in the middle of multiple choice questions?
o   How do you handle fair criticism?
o   How do you handle unjust criticism?
o   Can you handle confrontation, or do you run from it?
o   Was your sense of humor removed at birth or were you dropped on your head as a child?
o   Do you like to work alone when solving problems?
o   Are you more stimulated when working in a team when solving problems?
o   Are you a morning person?
o   Do you come alive in the afternoon/evening?
o   What do you do when you're not working?
o   Are you observant?
o   Do you find satisfaction in doing your job?
o   Do you feel appreciated and rewarded for doing your job?
o   Are you ambitious?
o   Do you study other people?
o   How do you define success?
o   Do you like to travel?
o   Have you made a list of the places in the world you would like to see?
o   Are you comfortable in other cultures?

- ○ Do you hate answering questions like these?
- ○ Can you stand on your feet and talk at the same time?

This list of questions could go on for several pages, and each of you can add other questions to it.

But I can guarantee you that two things will happen to you as you go through life:

1. Your answers to all of these questions will change over time, because
2. You will change over time.

The most important thing that you can do is to keep asking yourself these type of questions. You're trying to pin down the ever-shifting shadows defining who you really are, what you think, how you think, and how you interact with other people.

Early in my career, I had a job in New York City for a petrochemical company with plants in Texas. I would catch the early train on Monday morning so that I had time to read all the telexes (we had just retired our quill pens) from the plants detailing their current status and all the problems they had. I then summarized all the problems we were facing with production schedules, shipments, and meeting all the demands of the marketing department. My long list of problems looked especially daunting one particular morning and I was working for the best boss I have ever had. Through the cloud of cigar smoke, I can still see him leaning as far back as his chair would go, hands behind his head, a big grin on his face, both feet propped up on his desk, and saying, "Well, we are where we are. The only relevant question is what are we going to do about it." I have never forgotten that quote and have re-used and re-applied it many times over the years. It is still a crystal clear moment of clarity for me when I find myself immersed in a fog of details.

George Patton said that "A poor plan executed violently today is always better than the perfect plan done next week."

I attended a very small rural high school in Southern Ohio, all 12 grades in one building, 80 people in my graduating class, no football team. I played the last game of my basketball career at our fiercest rival and we lost. After the game, their coach, a massive man named Carroll Hawhee (tall, wide, deep booming voice, commanding presence) came up to me on the court, shook my hand, and said, "Son, you were a good high school basketball player, but you could have been better." "What do you mean, sir?", said I, because everyone called him sir. He said, "What were you supposed to be doing on the court?" I said." Play full court defense, get every offensive and defensive rebound that I could, set picks, make all my foul shots, never miss a layup." He said, "I saw you do all of that, to the best of your ability, but you could have done a lot more." I said, "What do you mean?" He said, "Why didn't you take more shots? Why didn't you over-play the right-handed players to force them to go to their left? Didn't you know that a missed shot taken from the left side of the basket will result in a rebound on the right side of the basket 75% of the time? The shots you did take had a flat trajectory. If you had put more arch on your shots, they would have had a much better chance of going in the basket." I said, "I was just doing what my coach told me to do." He said, "You absolutely should do that, but don't let other people put limits on what you can do in life. If you don't try, who knows what you might be able to achieve?"

Fourteen years later, my younger brother played for Coach Hawhee and heard the same speech many, many times.

There was also an occasion while my brother played for him when one of the players was caught with some drugs in his school locker. Coach Hawhee gathered the team together and said, "I'm leaving the room and you guys will determine his punishment." My brother said they all grew up that day.

Who are you?

What are you trying to accomplish?

You're burning daylight!

c. THE JOY OF PRODUCTIVE IDLENESS

The key to being good at whatever profession you are pursuing is to find time to do nothing, which sounds contradictory to our modern society's constant push to relentlessly stay busy, or at least give that appearance. Staying constantly busy is not to be confused with being productive or accomplishing anything of substance.

Just this morning, I saw a young man on a bicycle pedaling across 6 lanes of traffic, not at an intersection, while texting on his phone !

Our society worships people who appear industrious, but trying not to just stay busy would actually be much more productive. Avoiding *work* or the perception of *work* gives you the precious time to think. It sounds contradictory but you're actually wasting time if you can't find some time to waste !

Doing nothing may be absolutely the best thing to do with your time until you can figure out what to do. Mindlessly picking a random task to occupy your mind is mental laziness.

Set aside 15 minutes every day to just set and think (take it out of your lunch hour – you don't need an hour to eat lunch). When I worked in New York City, I would catch the train in Darien, CT and 55 minutes later I was in Grand Central Terminal (it's not a station). So I had nearly 2 hours every day to think, read, write, work, play bridge, play gin rummy, drink a Fosters (26 ounce can) in the evening, sleep, or some combination of the above. I treasured that time twice a day. You have a choice – you can bitch about the commute or you can put the time to good use. This was before cell phones so it was relatively quiet, except for the snorers.

Try this approach in your office:

1. Shut your door.
2. Turn off your phones.
3. Minimize all open sites on your computer screen.
4. Stare out your window at a distant tree or cloud and use that space between your ears.
5. Closing your eyes is OK but don't get caught sleeping.
6. Pick a problem.
7. Think about all the things you know and don't know about the problem.
8. Park the problem in your sub-conscious and let it marinate.
9. Think about the things that went right recently and why.
10. Think about the things that went wrong recently and why.

11. Think about what information you don't have (known unknowns).
12. Think about what information you don't know about and where you might find it (unknown unknowns); probably the toughest problem to solve.
13. Repeat process sometime in the evening, perhaps accompanied by an adult beverage.
14. Keep a daily diary – force yourself to make a daily accounting of your work life. It will be invaluable to you in the future.

Step back from a situation and really see what's in front of you:

- What's happening?
- What does it mean?
- Why is it happening?
- What's the message?
- What is it telling you?
- Walk around the situation and look at it from the other side – does it look different?
- What don't you see?
- What's missing that should be there?

Be thankful for the troubles of your job. They provide about half your income. Because if it were not for the things that go wrong, the difficult people you have to work with, and the problems and unpleasantness of your working day, someone could be found to handle your job for half of what you are being paid.

It takes intelligence, resourcefulness, patience, tact, and courage to meet the troubles of any job. That is why you hold your present job. And it may be the reason you aren't holding down an even bigger job.

If all of us would start looking for more troubles, and learn to handle them cheerfully and with good judgment as opportunities rather than as irritations, we would find ourselves getting ahead at a surprising rate. For it is a fact that there are plenty of big jobs waiting for people who aren't afraid of the troubles connected with them.

Henry Paulson went to Dartmouth College on a football scholarship playing offensive tackle. His first job after graduating was with Goldman Sachs, an investment banking firm in New York City. As a brand-new employee, he invited anyone in the bank to bring him problems. How do you react when you see or hear about a problem? Do many of us say to ourselves, "Thank God, that's not my problem." Firemen run towards fires. Policemen run towards trouble. Henry ran towards problems. He never played *Shoot the Messenger.* He didn't care where the problems were or how big or how small they were, and he was an excellent listener. He firmly believed that the sooner any problem was solved, the better off the company would be. Communication was very open as he had removed the fear from the conversation.

When Henry Paulson left the chairman's job at Goldman Sachs to become Secretary of the Treasury under President George W. Bush, he had $700 million in the bank, and he and his wife decided to donate it all to charity. "We're not going to spoil our kids by giving them piles of money."

Would you run towards problems?

d. CRITICAL THINKING

It's refreshing to take a positive approach to your job and employ "Critical Thinking", a concept you can Google on the Internet and which psychologists Carole Wade and Carol Tavris explained in 1990. Don't be misled by the word "critical" because they don't mean for it to be judgmental or taken negatively. They explain 8 elements of the process which will make you think you're in a detective show on TV, and it's an interesting parallel:

1. Ask questions. Be willing to wonder. What if?
2. Define the problem correctly; don't try to solve a symptom.
3. Examine the evidence: What do you know? What do you think you know? What don't you know?
4. Analyze your assumptions and your biases. We all have them, sometimes unconsciously.
5. Avoid emotional reasoning. Try making rational decisions.
6. Don't over-simplify. Inconvenient facts just won't go away.
7. Consider other interpretations. There are many shades of gray.
8. Tolerate uncertainty. The fastest route to an answer isn't always (and usually rarely) is the right or best answer. There are no blue ribbons for the person who is first to come up with an answer. Beware instant analyses – doubt pays dividends – hunches can be wrong – but learn to trust your gut – it's called experience.

Henry Evans, founder of Dynamic Results LLC, and author of "Winning With Accountability: The Secret Language of High

Performance Organizations" suggests banishing the following terms from all of your written and verbal communications:

- ASAP
- I'll do my best.
- I'll get right on it.
- The end of the day.
- Let's do something new and bold.
- Let's do a better job.
- Let's improve our service levels.
- Let's increase sales.
- Let's beat our competition to market.

All of the above terms are a "Glossary of Failure", murky language land mines that just lead to trouble because they aren't specific. And because they aren't specific, you've hamstrung yourself with your own words.

There are 4 pieces to the accountability puzzle:

1. Clearly stated expectations,
2. Specific date and time requirements,
3. A designated person or persons responsible for getting it done, and
4. Sharing results with everyone who needs to know.

Need help discovering the fuzzy terms you may be using? Ask the people you work with. Look at your past e-mails and see what potholes you have left on the information highway. We all do it ! But we all can recognize when we're not following the above accountability guidelines. Write them on a sticky note and put it on the edge of your computer screen as a reminder.

Rob Lebow of the Lebow Company in Bellevue, WA has developed a "Shared Values" program, where he sits down with the people in a company and they together write down the guiding principles that they want to follow in their work both with each other and with their clients. If you don't think about it, verbalize it, and write it down, how in the world do you ever expect to have a common value system that all of you can try to follow?

An example for one company looked like this:

- Treat each other with uncompromising truth, nicely
- Lavish trust on your co-workers
- Mentor each other unselfishly
- Listen carefully to new ideas, regardless of their origin
- Take careful risks for the sake of the organization
- Unselfishly give credit where it is due
- Don't cheat or lie – don't touch dishonest dollars
- Put the interests of others before your own interests.

Can you achieve all of these goals? A realistic answer is probably not, but you should have goals that you are striving towards every day. How else can you ever expect to improve?

e. READ EVERY DAY

- Know what's happening in the world and how those events affect your life and job?
- Don't just read things you agree with – challenge yourself
- Stretch your boundaries – get out of your rut

- Alternate reading fiction books with reading non-fiction books
- Mysteries teach problem solving and diagnostics
- Biographies are great teachers of how others have figured out their lives — examples for you

f. LISTEN TO MUSIC EVERY DAY

While you're reading every day, listen to music. It soothes your soul, especially after a rough day out there in the tough, sometimes un-forgiving real world.

g. PURSUIT OF PERFECTION

Many people have drunk the Kool-Aid and think they can achieve perfection if they just try hard enough. But many times that approach results in paralysis as you become afraid of doing anything for fear of making a mistake. If you live your life with this self-imposed limit, you will really limit what you can achieve. You can't be wrong if you don't move? Wrong, and that approach is self-defeating and works really well. Whether you have been conditioned by parents, relatives, peers, teachers, or bosses, you cannot be perfect. Get over yourself. Only one person in the world's history was perfect, so how audacious is it of you to think you can be perfect? Yes, have goals, objectives, and guidelines for acceptable behavior that you want to try to follow in your life, but stop beating yourself up ! Just think that if you magically achieved perfection, you've just broken even, there's nowhere to go from there. Much better to move forward, learn from your mistakes, and keep improving every day. Don't give up !

You will always miss 100% of the shots you don't take. Do you think Tiger Woods is the perfect golfer? Ask him ! Look at the relentless practice and changes he keeps making to his golf game to try and get better.

The point is to keep trying, because that's the only thing you can control, and the only thing you can constructively do. There are no legitimate excuses/reasons for not trying. Do you know the difference between an excuse and a reason: An excuse is when you don't want to do something; a reason is when you can't do something.

Emotional bankruptcy will be the only result of trying to be perfect.

h. RIPPLE EFFECT OF YOUR ACTIONS/ INACTIONS

Stop and think about the effects that you have on the world around you. Every word, every gesture, every action is perceived differently by all the people around you.

This morning's lesson came when I was driving down a six lane divided street here in Dallas. I had a roommate in college whose major was urban planning and his traffic engineering course was amazingly similar to a course I had taken called fluid mechanics, which was about the behavior of gases and liquids in piping systems. Traffic flow also has friction, choke points, pressure drops, and pressure increases. The driver who is on their phone (I believe men are worse than women) texting, weaving, slowing down, speeding up, making sudden stops and lane changes, is affecting all the other drivers around their vehicles, mostly mentally but sometimes physically. But this principle is also true for every interaction you have with other people.

Nothing would irritate me more than getting an e-mail from the person in the office next to my office. You're not communicating with me if all I see are words on an electronic screen. Get off your butt and come talk to me if you have something to say. I want to see your facial expressions, read your body language, feel your passion, and hear the volume and emphasis you place on certain words – now you're communicating !

There is even some hope that the interchange develops into an actual conversation. There is no hope if you're just staring at a screen. Do you know what the first conversation in the Bible was? Your first guess will probably be wrong – mine was.

One of my first bosses clued me in on the ripple effect of decisions – those made and those not made. Also, the effects may not be readily apparent or even immediate, as they may take some passage of time to reveal themselves. But every result is the product of an action or an inaction, and it's usually a series of events, not an isolated incident.

There is something in the human animal, let's call it ego, that much prefers praise to ridicule, that wants to be built up rather than torn down. We dislike scorn or censure (negative) and like validation or recognition (positive). I've been laughed at, scorned, ridiculed, derided, and lost several jobs, but it didn't stop me because I am extremely stubborn. Yes, it hurt, but it didn't stop me. It's no fun to be made a negative example just so someone else can feel good about themselves. A pessimist sees a room filled with horse manure and turns away disgusted. An optimist gets a shovel and starts digging – there's got to be a pony in there somewhere ! Don't allow anything to stop you – detours, yes – roadblocks, yes – but how to go over, under, around, or through them is the only relevant question.

Regardless of how small and trivial your job may seem to be in the grand scheme of things in the world, take pride in doing your job correctly, promptly, and well. An unseen ripple effect does move through the world whether you do your job poorly or whether you do it well.

i. YOUR PERSONAL WORK SPACE

Let's assume that you have a work space that you can call your own. It might be a table, a cubicle, or a room with a door, maybe even a window. How do you arrange it?

- We all collect mementoes, souvenirs, cartoons, pictures, toys, etc.
- Put all of that in a drawer or behind you. If you can see them, you'll get distracted and start thinking about them.
- Do you have a 2DO list? Put it in a drawer.
- Focus only on what is in front of you that you need to complete your task
- Don't answer the phone. People will leave voice mail which you can respond to later. If it's really important, you will get visitors.

- Minimize your e-mail system so you can't see it. Very few e-mails are really urgent or that important. They're mostly CYA or FYI – review them later.
- If you have a door, shut it.

None of the above should be taken as anti-social, un-cooperative, aloof, or not playing well with others. You need to train your co-workers to respect your privacy for chunks of time so that you can get your work done. Maybe some of your behavior will rub off on them !

John Cheever was a famous author in the middle of the last century. He lived in an apartment building in New York City and every morning he would get cleaned up, dress in a suit and tie, and take the elevator to the basement. He was going to work. He had a table with a typewriter on it that faced a blank wall. He would strip down to his underwear and type all morning. At noon, he would get dressed and spend the rest of the day drinking, but that was his method for getting his work done. It worked for him. You don't get Pulitzer Prizes out of Crackerjack boxes.

Ernest Hemingway had a typewriter sitting on top of a bookcase. He typed and re-typed standing up and would not allow himself to stop until he had 10 good pages each day. He would leave the last sentence unfinished so he had somewhere to start the next day and thus avoided writer's block. He won a Pulitzer Prize and a Nobel Prize. His method worked for him.

John Grisham was a young lawyer in Oxford, MS who wanted to write novels. He put a small table in his utility room between the washer and dryer, set up a small computer, and wrote from 5AM to 7AM every morning. Then he went to his day job. His first book, "A Time To Kill", didn't do well (I thought it was great) and he was selling copies out of the trunk of his car. You may have heard of his second book, "The Firm." His method worked for him.

Daniel Silva and Nelson DeMille, more current authors (I highly recommend both of them), write their novels in pencil on yellow legal pads and then have someone else put them into electronic form. They both say they need to see words on paper to envision how the story will go. Neither uses an outline – it's all in their heads. Their methods work for them.

The point of the above examples is to find a method that works for you – that allows you to get your work done efficiently.

j. PLANNING YOUR WORK

So you've got your own work space – how do you go about doing your work?

If you just react to the daily demands other people place on you, it will be chaos, and you'll just respond to the loudest screams. You will work as if on remote control. You need to try to impose some order or you will be hopelessly lost. Try this:

- Respond first to all requests from people above you in the organization by asking when and in what form do they require answers. Be sure you understand what they are asking for.
- From your hidden 2DO list in your desk drawer, what is the most important item that needs work – do that.

- Take the smallest sticky note you can find, tear it in half, and write on it what your most important task is. Put that note on the top of your computer monitor. Focus on it.

- If you have geographic clients, start with those east of you and work your way west. For example, when I worked at the consulting company, clients in the Middle East had gone home for the day by the time I got to work. So I would answer European clients (and maybe get responses while I was still in the office), then start in the Eastern time zone of the US and work my way west. By the time my day was ending, the clients in the Far East were just starting their next work day. Then I would answer the Middle East clients last so they would have responses when they got to their offices on their next business day.

- My general rule, regardless of time of day or day of week, was to always be working on what I thought was the most important problem at that point in time. If I was wrong, I was sure to get lots of help. Experience will guide your decisions on what is most important, but that rule proved best for me.

- You can waste a lot of time making lists, rating projects by importance, and trying to plan your work. I think your time is better spent actually doing some work.

k. MANAGEMENT TIME – WHO'S GOT THE MONKEY?

The above title is the most reprinted article in the history of the Harvard Business Review, from the November–December 1974 issue, by William Oncken Jr. and Donald L. Wass, of the management consulting firm The William Oncken Company of Texas. It is still just as relevant today as when it was printed 44 years ago, and I think it important enough to quote it in its entirety. Please see Appendix E.

Why is it that managers are typically running out of time while their subordinates are typically running out of work? In this article, they explore the meaning of management time as it relates to the interaction between managers and their bosses, their own peers, and their subordinates. Not only was it fascinating, I could see it being played out in the relationships I observed in several of the companies where I have worked. But if you haven't stopped and thought about what is going on, you may not realize how people hamstring each other in their daily work lives.

1. GOD GIVES POP QUIZZES

I look at problems, both large and small, that pop up in my life as God testing me by giving me a pop quiz, sometimes several in one day. They are a great teacher of patience, but sometimes the lessons are really hard. Just assume that they're coming, you just don't know when or why.

The person many consider to be the greatest golfer ever, Jack Nicklaus, said that he always assumed he was going to get an unpleasant surprise on one hole in a round of golf. He never knew when, or how, or where, or why, but out of 18 holes, something was going to jump up and bite him – a bad bounce, a tree in his line, a spike mark on a green, a trap that he didn't get out of, a poor swing, a bad decision, etc. He planned on something happening, so he didn't let it upset him and played the other 17 holes as well as he could. They were all pop quizzes in his chosen profession as a professional golfer.

I can imagine God getting bored, nudging Jesus in the ribs, and saying, "Let's see how this silly human handles this problem ! And this one. And this one. And They sit back and chuckle. Can you hear Them? You're allowed to laugh back !

How do you handle pop quizzes? Cursing, groaning, complaining, why me? why now? It's a learning opportunity. Good fortune is God smiling at you. Misfortune is not God frowning at you, He just didn't smile. Bad luck is not punishment, it's just another test. It's just your turn. You're being trained. Brush it off and move on. Think of it as good luck is just around the corner.

M. HOW DO YOU DEFINE YOUR BUSINESS?

Let's say you're a dentist and have a dental office with a receptionist, chair-side assistants, and a dental hygienist. If you define your business as filling cavities, pulling teeth, getting people out of pain, and making dentures, you'll soon go broke.

However, if you define your business as offering oral hygiene, preventive maintenance, teaching people how to care for their teeth, how to recognize problems, and how to have a great smile, you will be very busy.

Steve Jobs re-imagined his business beyond the simple Mac computer and changed the world.

Southwest Airlines started out with 2 airplanes, declared that they were a transportation company, and their competition was the bus company. They offered cheap flights, frequent flights, quick turnarounds, friendly service, and kept their planes in the air 12 hours a day.

What is your company trying to do?

Make a profit? Wrong answer.

Your goal is to serve your clients.

The rest will follow.

n. HOW DO YOU DEFINE YOUR JOB?

- Where does your group fit in the organization?
- Where do you fit in your group?
- How do you get the information that you need?
- What do you do with the information you receive?
- Are you passive or proactive?
- Do you wait for assignments or go looking for things to do?
- When given work, do you ask questions so that you understand what is required, when it is required, and the method to use to report the results of your work?
- Do you stop there?
- Do you think about the implications of your work? What messages does it send? What else could you do with it?
- Can you analyze what you have done, so far, predict other problems, and go ahead and solve those problems?

- Think it all the way through.
- What is stopping you?
- Think about what you are doing – don't just do the minimum.
- Don't let fear paralyze you.
- You don't learn anything from your successes – they just validate what you already know.
- You will gain great experience from screwing things up.
- Start a project by visualizing what the final report will look like and work towards that.
- Don't spend a lot of time creating a plan or outline or schedule when you could be working.

Bear Bryant, the famous football coach at the University of Alabama, went to his bench during a game and said, "Smith, can you do a better job than Jones is doing in there?" "I can try, coach." "Sit back down, Jones is trying."

o. HUMOR IN BUSINESS

Look for it every day. It's all around you.

I have one infallible indicator that has worked for me all over the world. I would watch and listen to the people from the security guard or receptionist all the way to the big boss. If I saw and heard humor, if the people were razzing each other, if the needle was out and they were joking around with each other, I knew people were getting along with each other and that there was open communication without fear. This also correlated with the performance of the facility. The opposite was also always true.

Look at humor as the lubricant that keeps the wheels of industry turning.

Victor Borge: "Laughter is the shortest distance between 2 people."

Find ways to use humor. Before the start of every presentation or seminar or when showing up at a place I had never been before, I would tell myself the funniest joke I could remember. Some of them were not rated PG or *ready for prime time* but they would make me chuckle, and that was the whole point. I could then present a smiling, relaxed, and confident appearance, ready for anything anyone could throw at me.

Self-deprecating humor is priceless, and you have a great reservoir to draw from, because you made yourself the target in front of the whole audience. Now they can laugh and relax. You can now connect with them and not be viewed as lecturing or talking down to them.

When Bob Hope was on his deathbed, his wife Delores was talking with him about the various places in Hollywood where he could be buried. He looked at her and said, "Surprise me."

If I had something I needed to get done, and didn't want to be disturbed, I would tape the following sign on the outside of my closed door:

- I can only please one person per day.
- Today is not your day.
- Tomorrow doesn't look good either.

p. WHEN INSULTS HAD CLASS

There are times and places when nothing will fill the hole in a conversation or in your ongoing struggle with the world like a well-placed and eloquent insult. Many famous people have labored very hard on your behalf and I have gathered a few of my favorites for your edification:

- A member of Parliament to Benjamin Disraeli, Prime Minister of England: "Sir, you will either die on the gallows or of some unspeakable disease." "That depends Sir," said Disraeli, "On whether I embrace your policies or your mistress."
- Moses Hadas: "Thank you for sending me a copy of your book. I'll waste no time reading it."
- Count Talleyrand: "To avoid being called a flirt, she always yielded instantly."
- A grande dame approached Sir Winston Churchill at a cocktail party and exclaimed, "Sir Winston, you are drunk !" He replied, "And madam, you are ugly. But in the morning, I shall be sober."
- Clarence Darrow: "I have never killed a man, but I have read many obituaries with great pleasure."
- Forrest Tucker: "He loves nature in spite of what it did to him."
- Andrew Lang: "He uses statistics as a drunken man uses lamp posts- for support rather than for illumination."
- William Faulkner about Ernest Hemingway: "He has never been known to use a word that might send a reader to the dictionary."
- Groucho Marx: "I've had a perfectly wonderful evening, but I'm afraid this wasn't it."

- Winston Churchill: "He has all the virtues I dislike and none of the vices I admire."
- Mark Twain: "I didn't attend the funeral, but I sent a nice letter saying I approved of it."
- Oscar Wilde: "He has no enemies, but is intensely disliked by his friends."
- Billy Wilder: "He has Van Gogh's ear for music."
- Stephen Bishop: "I feel so miserable without you, it's almost like having you here."
- John Bright: "He is a self-made man and worships his creator."
- Irvin S. Cobb: "I've just learned about his illness. Let's hope it's nothing trivial."
- George Bernard Shaw to Winston Churchill: "I am enclosing 2 tickets to the first night of my new play. Bring a friend, if you have one." Churchill's response: "Cannot possibly attend first night; will attend second night, if there is one."
- Samuel Johnson: "He is not only dull himself, he is the cause of dullness in others."
- Paul Keating: "He is simply a shiver looking for a spine to run up."
- Walter Kerr: "He had delusions of adequacy."
- Mark Twain: "Why do you sit there looking like an envelope without any address on it?"
- Mae West: "His mother should have thrown him away and kept the stork."
- Oscar Wilde: "Some cause happiness wherever they go; others, whenever they go."
- Unknown: "My wife ran off with my best friend and I miss him."

- Mac Davis: "Oh Lord, it's hard to be humble, when I'm perfect in every way. It's hard to look in the mirror, cause I get better looking each day."
- Oscar Wilde: "Only a mediocre person is at his best all the time."

q. WHEN BOREDOM STRIKES YOU

It's going to happen to everyone, but what do you do about it?

- Don't panic.
- Don't be afraid of going down into a mental rabbit hole.
- Go to Starbucks and chill out.
- Take a walk.
- Don't pester anyone who looks like they're working.
- Talk to someone you don't know in another department. They will be happy to talk about themselves (it's their favorite subject). Ask how you and your department can help them and their department do their job better. You just made an invaluable ally.
- Think about a problem.
- Try out different approaches or different methodologies to solving problems.
- Solicit help from mentors and chew the fat with them.
- Read something new that is relative to your job.
- Ask for something new to work on.

r. THE PURSUIT OF HAPPINESS

I believe that many people think of psychology in a negative sense as it is seen as dealing with emotional or mental problems. I would rather think of it in a positive sense as presented in "The Pursuit of Happiness", an article by Tracy Staton in the

American Way magazine of 1 October 2008. A friend of mine says that happiness comes from having low expectations in life – sarcastic but maybe true in some cases. I quote the article in its entirety in Appendix G for your consideration.

VIII

WHY YOU MUST UNDERSTAND YOUR OWN LIMITATIONS

a. CIRCLES, FEEDBACK LOOPS & LIMITS

When I was working for the consulting company in Dallas, I had gone to a small town in the Midwestern US to visit an oil refinery and was talking to my contact about his potential interest in working for our company. He made the observation that everything he did in his life was within 5 miles of his house: work, schools, stores, church, restaurants, doctors, hospitals, etc. I was struck by a similarity: I too lived in a similar sized circle, except my circle was in a very big town and his circle encompassed his entire town.

One of the most interesting statistics I have ever read is that two-thirds of the people in the US live within 50 miles of where they graduated from high school. If you don't believe that, the sample size you're thinking about is too small. I believe I can rationalize that statistic if you can accept a sequence of events: getting out of school, getting a job, getting married, starting a family, staying near family and in-laws, and settling into the same pattern you have maybe unconsciously seen with all of your friends and relatives. Let me hasten to add that I'm not being judgmental – there is absolutely nothing wrong with following that type of life pattern. Statistics say that lots of people do that. But allow me to offer two other concepts which may not be apparent to you if you're in one of the above circles.

Regardless of how you receive information (radio, TV, paper, internet), you are being inundated with *bad news*. All media is fighting to get your attention so that you will get the latest scintillating *just-have-to-know-and-be-up-to-date* tidbit of new stuff so that you will coincidentally notice the flood of advertising that is surrounding you. Lacking facts, they will create stories based on *what-if* or speculation. *If it bleeds, it leads* is the mantra of every form of media because that's their job, to get you to pay attention. I'm just asking that you be aware of what's happening because you're inside a *feedback loop*.

It's very easy to become conditioned by the information we see and hear, and perhaps unconsciously, retreat to our comfort zone, that safe familiar circle where most of live our lives. When you are repeatedly told how bad and scary the big outside world is, you cannot help but be affected by what you see and hear. That's the definition of a feedback loop and you should realize what is happening to you. I didn't say it was all bad, it just is.

Which brings us to the topic of *limits_–* what are they, who decides what they are, what do you do about them, how do you go around, over, or through the limits you encounter in life? The short answer is that it is all up to you. Not making a decision is making a decision by default. Who you gonna call? Superman is on vacation, Spiderman is out of town, and Batman ain't answering his batphone ! Feeling lonely yet?

Physical limits – only a very few people are 7 feet tall and can dunk from the free throw line, so an NBA career probably isn't going to happen for you. A tiny percentage of people make a living as a professional athlete, so let's think about other limits.

Intelligence limits – if you want to pursue a profession that requires a certain level of proficiency such as teachers, engineers, lawyers, doctors, and many other professions, that may require more brainpower than you have, so you might have to alter your sights a little. Nothing against you personally – the person finishing last in his class at medical school is still called *Doctor.*

Emotional limits – you need to decide whether your internal feelings (I'm struggling here to describe something many of us have trouble verbalizing) will allow you to be a counselor, psychologist, or cleric, someone able to sit down with another person and discuss emotions, feelings, prejudices, desires, or relationships. Call it *Touchy-Feely* if that helps you get a grasp on the concept, but there is no shame in admitting that you'd just rather not go there.

Economic limits – you may find some avenues out of reach because you just don't have the money to pursue them. But you might be surprised to find out that there is help out there that you didn't know about. Sports psychologists have long had a maxim that, "If you didn't achieve a goal, it's because you didn't try hard enough." Say your goal is to make 5 basketball free throws in a row. When you achieve that goal, set a new goal of 10. Then a new goal of 20, etc. Keep pushing yourself, and you can achieve much more than you originally thought you could.

There are probably many other types of limits you may have encountered or can think of, but all of these limits have one thing in common:

You set your own limits, either by conscious choice, or by allowing others to set them for you

- You are the only one who can decide the work you like or want to do
- You are the one who can choose to be happy or unhappy
- You don't know what your limits are until you bump up against them
- You will find that other people want to help you determine your limits, but they can be wrong
- If you think you're in a box, *You Are* ! Because you put yourself there. You defined the length, width, and height of the box. Only you can change the dimensions. Start asking questions.

b. THE POLISH KAYAKER

A fascinating story in the New York Times magazine of 25 March 2018 describes Aleksander Doba, a mechanical engineer who works at a petrochemical plant in Police, Poland.

He talked about the *Tyranny of Politeness* that occurred during the courtship of his future wife. His future mother–in–law had him over for dinner and served duck's blood soup. A guest is supposed to compliment everything he is fed. To avoid the nightmare of conformity, and knowing that if he didn't speak up, he would have to eat it at every future meal, Aleksander said, "This is a good soup. It looks good. It smells good, probably everybody likes it. But this specific soup, I don't like." His future mother-in-law was shocked, but got over it, and never fixed that soup for him again.

His wife works for social services in the Polish government, his children were grown, and he had no hobbies. A friend asked him to join the kayak club at their plant, so he took his first kayak trip, and fell in love. It keeps him out of his wife's hair. He paddled down the river to the Baltic Sea and back. Then he traveled the entire perimeter of the Baltic Sea. Then he traveled the entire western coast of Norway, bottom to top to bottom. Then he designed his own kayak and has now paddled across the Atlantic Ocean 3 times: there is a northern route, a central route, and a southern route to South America. He has a GPS and a satellite phone on his kayak so he can always be found, except for the day when they stopped working. Nothing he could do about it so he just kept paddling. His wife realized she hadn't heard from him in a while, started checking, and realized that the credit card that paid the fees had expired, so she reinstated it and checked in with him. He was fine except he was getting annoyed by ships that kept trying to rescue him.

He was asked what happens when he has a crisis when out on the ocean when he's all alone. He calmly said that he had had many crises, but he just re-imagines a crisis as an opportunity. "As it's now an opportunity, I can imagine myself as a hero, so I give myself control, and handle the crisis." An example he gave was when he lost his sea anchor, which was like a cloth sail that trailed in the water behind his kayak and kept him pointed in a certain direction, like perpendicular to the direction of the waves. He was in 50 foot waves, had to crawl out on the back of his kayak, and rig up a temporary sea anchor until the storm passed. If he had not done this, the waves would have beaten his kayak to pieces.

The person who wrote the article said that although Aleksander is 71, he looks like he was put together from different kits. His skin looks 71. His chest looks 50. His shoulders and forearms look 30. His hands are about 3 times the size of normal humans. His hair and beard look like a Michelangelo painting of God.

c. HITCHHIKING THE WORLD

The same magazine had an article about a hitchhiker, not just your ordinary run-of-the-mill hitchhiker. He has walked from the North Pole to the South Pole through the Americas. He has walked from Portugal to Shanghai, across all of Europe and Asia. His girlfriend has now joined him and they both just carry a backpack. He has never had a problem, has been fed and housed countless times, and remains mystified, surprised, and grateful for the continual kindness of strangers.

The point of the article was that he had not set any geographical limits on himself. He literally wanted to see the world and is still doing it.

He also talked about a feedback loop that tells us the world is much worse than it actually is, and we trick ourselves into believing it to be true, when it's not. We've conditioned ourselves to believe a false narrative because what we see is not an average or even a range of expected outcomes, but rather the outer limits of our reality – limited by what we have seen and heard.

Let's take an example from current events. Why is there widespread appeal for President Trump's idea of building a wall between our country and Mexico? Forget politics for a moment. Here's a problem with a simple proposed solution — build a wall to keep *them* out. But the vast majority of our population is so stupid, in the literal sense of the word, that they can't appreciate the physical, fiscal, practical problems associated with such an endeavor. The notion of building a barrier that extends for 1,954 miles (that people will go under, around, or through) is just ludicrous to me.

But it's not ludicrous if you live in a tiny circle in the world outside of which you have never ventured. It's a simplistic presentation of a *problem* with a simplistic *solution* which a lot of people can support because they can't envision or appreciate the amount of time and money, the practical problems, the lack of efficiency of the *solution*, nor the rational justification for such an idea, and don't have a clue about what a 1,954 mile long wall would look like. It's simply beyond their conception.

IX

WHY YOU MUST CHANGE WHEN YOU START WORKING

a. COMPETITION

Credit for this topic goes to Kevin Proops, a co-worker at my last company, resulting from a conversation we had one day. If you get nothing else out of this book, *please* get and hold on to these 2 concepts.

Regardless of how advanced your level of education or training, you eventually have to work for a living. You can't live in your parent's basement or your aunt's attic forever, and need at least enough money for food, clothing, and shelter. Cars and beer costs extra. But you must accept 2 premises, and you don't have a choice on either one:

PREMISE # 1: Until you get a job, your entire focus has been on *competition*, more knowledge, and a better understanding of how the world works. Your whole future had shrunk to getting the best grades you can, so you can get into the best school, get the best job, get the highest salary, etc.

b. COOPERATION/COLLABORATION

PREMISE # 2: But now you need to change your focus ! It is imperative that you begin to *cooperate and collaborate* with your co-workers. You need to make this change because the problems are too large and complex for one person to be able to solve them alone. How would you know what pieces of information you were missing? What are the unintended consequences of any actions you plan to take? You don't know everything, and the sooner you accept that premise, the better off for everyone. I have seen many very smart people go down in flames because they tried to do things by themselves. *Doesn't play well with others* applies equally well in the sandbox or playground as well as it does in a work environment. I don't care if you're sweeping floors at McDonalds, mowing lawns, or running a Fortune 500 company.

What will happen if you try to stay in your old, comfortable competitive mode and try to gather all the glory for yourself? First, your co-workers will hate your guts. OK, maybe you'll just severely irritate them, but they will be reluctant to communicate with you or to work with you because they know you are just trying to claim all of the credit with the boss. Occasionally, that strategy will work, but most bosses wouldn't be bosses if they couldn't see right through that charade. That's why they're bosses.

Cooperation and collaboration takes lots of practice because we are all naturally competitive. Maybe it's a leftover trait from the cavemen or it was learned through athletics, but competition is not a bad thing by itself. I think that learning to work with others must first involve developing *trust*. If you're going to let your guard down, share ideas, listen to each other, solve problems, and implement viable solutions to the *way things have always been done*, you and the people you work with must develop trust in each other. Second, you must *respect* each other. Early in his career, General George Patton would gather his troops together and say, "OK, the stripes are off (meaning rank didn't matter). Tell me what's going on, what are the problems, what's not getting done, what do you need from me, what other units of the army are giving you grief – talk to me. And nothing goes beyond this room !" I think Patton saw his role as a problem solver, and he couldn't do that if he didn't know what the problems were.

I have taught many seminars all over the world and the first thing I would always say, after good morning and welcome, was that for today and tomorrow, there will be no such thing as a dumb question. If it's important enough for you to think it, speak up at any time, because then it's important for me to answer it right now. Don't worry if it's off topic or something we talked about yesterday. If you're like me, you might forget if you wait. I lied, the very first thing I would point out, after welcome, was the location of the rest rooms. It's difficult to hear when your high-level alarm is going off. Even then, I was somewhere in the Middle East when someone, quite seriously, asked me what a rest room was. They thought I meant somewhere to go take a nap. I once again re-learned the lesson of English being a second language and not recognizing that a phrase common in our culture would be confusing in another culture. So from then on, I carefully used the word *toilet* to avoid any confusion. Which brings me to another story about toilets in the Middle East, but I'll save it for later.

X

HOW TO WORK WITH OTHER PEOPLE

a. COEXISTING WITH COWORKERS

You didn't pick them, so you have to learn to live with them !

Let's say you're just out of school and starting to work at your first job, or maybe you're starting a new job. You're the new kid on the block, a stranger in a strange town, just trying to figure out what the hell is going on. How do you behave? The first thing you should do is smile at everyone. They will all wonder what you have been up to, but more importantly you won't appear threatening to the status quo, nor to them personally. Bring donuts. Everybody loves donuts.

POP QUIZ: What is the origin of the handshake?

SECOND POP QUIZ: Why do the Brits drive on the other side of the road?

People will be more willing to work with you and co-operate with you when they don't sense danger. Think of the opposite effect: they won't co-operate or communicate with you if they sense danger or risk to their status or their careers.

What types of people should you avoid or at least be tiptoeing around when starting a new job? Steve Strauss in USA Today on 18 May 2018 describes 6 types of people who will either impede your work (actively or passively) or get in your head enough to distract you and keep you from putting forth your best effort. They are all *LOSERS* ! But get your defenses built ahead of time so that you can recognize them and practice the Boy Scout motto: Be Prepared !

1. *NOPEYS* – This is the person who always says NO to any idea, suggestion, or new concept just because they didn't think of it. They go on a verbal offensive – attack everybody else because they have nothing to offer. They imagine that they've taken the high ground by being the first to oppose everything, creating a false self image of power, and eventually find themselves all alone most of the time, which can really be irritating. Carry a salt shaker with you and don't be intimidated or fall for their act.

2. **PIG** – Did someone eat your lunch? Leave dirty dishes in the sink? Explode something in the microwave? Leave something disgusting in the refrigerator that is growing in interesting colors and emitting heretofore unknown aromas? Call them out and shame them into acting like adults and cleaning up their own messes. Everyone else will appreciate your speaking out and you will quickly make a bunch of new friends.

3. *PETTY THIEF* – Who gave them the license to pilfer the supply cabinet to fill all of their and their family's needs? Paper, pencils, pens, and every other

type of office supplies suddenly grow legs and walk home with them every evening in pockets, purses, briefcases, backpacks, etc. Don't they understand the basic economic principle that the company ends up paying for all the goodies they take out the door?

4. *GOSSIP* – Nothing destroys morale, hurts feelings, and disrupts working relationships faster and more efficiently than tongues wagging behind people's backs. Don't listen to it, don't repeat any of it, and try to ignore it. All they're trying to do is to distract you from getting your work done while they're not getting their own work done. Who do you think comes out ahead? The usual result is to tear someone else down so that they feel better about themselves. Does that sound like the yellow brick road to success?

5. *CLUELESS* – Talks too loud, showers infrequently, deodorant is failing, mouthwash isn't cutting it (Clint Eastwood quote from a "Dirty Harry" movie), arrives late, leaves early, long winded, leaves no thought unspoken – no silence unbroken, uses paragraphs for bullet points, disorganized, rambling writer and speaker. Who wants to work with such a person? Better question is who hired this person.

6. *CHEAPSKATE* – Short arms and deep pockets. At lunch, asks if anyone has change for a $100 bill. How do you have the most drinks and the most expensive entree and put the least money in the communal pot to pay for the joint meal?

Not every company has all of these *LOSERS* because they are not productive and someone will fire them. But learn to recognize them because you may have to work with some of them, for awhile.

b. THE ILLUSION OF THE FAMILIAR

Let's say that you go into the place where you are working and this is what you see:

- Floor is dirty
- Some lights don't work
- Some people are late to work
- Some people don't show up at all
- Trashcans weren't emptied last night
- So-and-so is out sick, again
- Your computer won't boot up, again
- The break room has dirty dishes in the sink
- Phones are ringing but not being answered
- Several intense solitaire games are in progress
- The person who got the last cup of coffee didn't make a new pot
- Worse, the coffee pot was left on the burner and now has an asphalt coating in the bottom
- Something has exploded inside the microwave
- Something in the refrigerator smells like it is way past its expiry date

But you've become numb to all of the above because it's what you're used to seeing every day, it's become normal and *familiar*. You may even think that this is how all workplaces operate because you've never seen any other workplaces. Nothing surprises you. But, you don't know what *good* looks like. It's familiar to you, but it doesn't have to be that way !

I spent 25 years working all over the world for a consulting company that helped petroleum refineries operate more efficiently. Your knowledge and understanding of refineries can approach zero and you can still appreciate the absurdity of one refinery that I visited:

- I could smell and hear the refinery before I got to the security gate
- I had to watch a 15 minute safety video, take a 2 page quiz, and get a perfect score to get a visitor's pass
- Lacking a perfect score, I would get the opportunity to watch the video again
- No one was allowed on foot inside the refinery because it was enveloped in a cloud of steam condensation from all of the steam leaks in the refinery (it was a cold day)
- I traveled in a pickup with a 5 mile per hour speed limit (so we wouldn't run into anything)
- The smell was from all the leaks in the process units
- The noise was from the flares burning off excess gases, sounding like a freight train
- The noise was also from compressors gargling their bearings
- You could have put bleachers in the control rooms and maintenance shops to accommodate all the people standing around

When I started asking questions, it was quickly apparent that nothing unusual was happening – the refinery always looked, smelled, and sounded that way – it was *familiar*. But it doesn't have to be this way ! I have visited many refineries that were the exact sensual opposites. I've seen some that could be in *Architectural Digest*.

Here's a take home quiz: What does your workplace look like? Does anything seem wacky? Does anyone care?

c. PRACTICE ACTIVE LISTENING

Are you really listening, or just waiting for your turn to talk, or interrupt before the other person is through talking?

Never ask a question unless you are willing to listen to the answer.

Talking is a way to communicate ideas and here are some killer techniques to avoid when you are supposed to be listening. It's going to take you some practice to begin to listen well.

1. **Judging**
   "Well, what did you do this time?"

   "Tell me exactly how you did it (and I'll tell you where you screwed it up !)

   "You really look mad (sad, glad, etc.) today."

2. **Giving Advice**
   "Cheer up."

   "Next week, everything will be all right."

   "Here's the way to solve your problem (Dummy, why can't you do it yourself?"

3. **Questioning** (for diagnosis or as a guide for giving advice)

   "Have you tried to do it this way?"

   "Why did you do it that way?"

   "What answers have you tried?"

4. **How to Keep the Other Person Talking**
   "Go on."

   "That's interesting."

   "Oh?"

   "Let's hear about it."

   Silence.

Lean towards other person and raise your eyebrows.

If you try practicing any of these skills, please do so in a safe place. Practice only with people who are OK with the practice. Telling others that you are trying to improve your listening skills might help.

Remember that it is a proven fact that no one can talk and hear at the same time !

We all observe verbal and non-verbal communications. Which do we pay attention to?

Let's agree to follow and practice the following 8 suggestions for *Active Listening.*

1. When I ask you to listen to me and you start giving me advice, you have not done what I asked.
2. When I ask you to listen to me and you begin to tell me why I shouldn't feel that way, you are trampling on my feelings.
3. When I ask you to listen to me and you try to solve my problems, you have failed me.
4. Listen. All I ask is that you listen. Not talk or do – just listen.
5. When you do something for me that I can and need to do for myself, you contribute to my fear and weakness and ignorance.
6. Realize, please, that no matter how irrational and stupid I may sound, your listening helps me understand and make sense of myself.
7. Perhaps that's why prayer works so well for some people. God listens and doesn't give advice or try to fix things. He also answers every prayer – sometimes the answer is NO.
8. So, please just listen to me. And if you want to talk, wait a minute for your turn, and then I will listen to you. That's what friends are for.

d. WHY DO WE HAVE POLICIES & PROCEDURES?

It didn't happen all at once – it was an evolution. Imagine someone confronted with a problem or a situation or even a messy confrontation that they had never seen before. What to do? How do the people involved reach a conclusion or at least a consensus where everyone may not have gone away jumping for joy, but they could at least live with the results.

So time marches on and the very same or a very similar situation occurs again. And we all look around and ask ourselves how we handled the situation before. Bart Simpson's greatest contribution to American thinking then occurs, *DUH* ! Gee why don't we handle this situation the same way we did it last time? So that's why there's a flat spot on everyone's forehead !

Thus, a *policy* is born. It defines how we as an organization will react and not spend time and energy re-solving the same problem over and over again. We avoid bucking every problem up through all the layers of the organization until someone makes a decision for us. Think of a policy as a decision-making tool so you have some written guidance on how to handle a problem. Unfortunately, the policies get engraved on stone tablets and preserved for posterity. They get mounted in office lobbies and company headquarters and are worshipped by newbies to the organization. They even morph into "mission statements" that are so bland that they're not worth the paper they're printed on (kind of like a QJ doubleton in a bridge hand).

The biggest danger in slavishly following policies is that organizations forget the circumstances under which the policies were originally created. Circumstances change. Economics change. Markets change. We learn more, as an organization, about our suppliers, clients, and customers. Some organizations get lazy and forget how to think and the default button is to just follow the policy. Keep the car in the middle of the road between the ditches and I can't get blamed for anything that happens, I was just following the policy. It's safe.

Please don't take me wrong. Correctly written and applied, policies can save a bunch of a lot of people's time. Foolishly followed policies, applied without critical thinking and no individuals brave enough to ask a bunch of *stupid* questions, can quickly lead to disasters.

Let me give you an example using the *Swiss Cheese* theory of accident prevention. You can't see through the holes in several layers of Swiss cheese unless the layers are rearranged to line up the slices so that the holes coincide. Think of these layers of cheese as preventing accidents. A true story of an airplane flight follows:

An airline mechanic gets into a fight with his wife, has a few too many, sleeps poorly on the couch, and shows up late for work the next morning with a large hangover. The pilot, who had many fewer flight hours than the co-pilot, but was a great politician, had leap-frogged the co-pilot into the left-hand seat of the plane. The co-pilot, violating several company policies, had been out partying the night before with the stewardesses and showed up at the airport with a large bottle of aspirin and the largest cup of coffee that Starbucks could sell him. He stumbled going into the cockpit, spilled the entire cup of coffee all over the instrument panel of the plane, and soaked all of the control systems. Guess which maintenance mechanic was sent to the plane? Under pressure to get the plane in the air as quickly as his hangover would allow, the mechanic took apart the instrument panel, and thought he had cleaned up all of the coffee. He missed one drop. The plane takes off and encounters a large bank of thunderstorms. The pilot decides to turn left around a large thunderhead, and as he does, he sees a flashing red light indicating that the left engine is on fire. The standard policy in this case was to shut down the engine that was on fire. If the pilot had done that, with the right engine still under full power, the plane would have gone into a spin and crashed. The co-pilot, who knew by the seat of his pants that both engines were running with full power and could see that the plane had the proper attitude versus the horizon, took the controls away from the pilot, ignored the signal of a fire (remember the one drop of coffee?), restarted the left engine and flew the plane safely through the thunderstorms. Sadly, the co-pilot was written up for violating company policy and was fired. Narrow-minded idiots !

The point of the story is to understand how all the holes in the layers of Swiss cheese had to align for this event to occur. The last preventive layer was the more experienced co-pilot, who if he had followed the policy, would have died along with everyone else on the plane.

But human beings, being political animals, can screw up anything. A brief fable, unknown origin, may prove to be illuminating:

> "In the beginning was the plan, and then came the assumptions, and the assumptions were without form, and the plan was completely without substance, and darkness fell upon the face of the workers.

> And the workers spake unto their supervisors saying, "It is a crock of BS, and it stinketh."

And the supervisor went to his area supervisor, and sayeth, "It is a pail of dung, and none may abide the odor thereof."

And the area supervisor went to the production manager and sayeth, "It is a container of excrement, and it is very strong, and none here can abide it."

And the production manager went to the assistant area manager and sayeth, "It is a vessel of fertilizer, and none can abide the strength."

> And the assistant area manager went to the area manager and sayeth, "It contains that which aids plant growth, and it is very strong."

> And the area manager went to the director and sayeth, "It promoteth growth, and it is very powerful."

> And the director went to the chairman and sayeth, "This powerful new plan will actively promote the growth and efficiency of the company, and this operation in particular."

> And the chairman looked upon the plan and saw that it was good.

> And the plan became POLICY ! Sound familiar?

Okay, now you've got *policies*. What do you do with these new-born creations? The next logical step would be to create *procedures*, which ideally should carry out the original intent of the policies. Well-meaning and good-hearted people try to write down how the policies will be implemented via instructions, decision trees, handbooks, logic maps, rules, and any other device known to man (and woman) to illustrate what actions should be taken.

But there are pitfalls in blindly following procedures, chief among them is the avoidance of any blame being assigned for mistakes. *Hey, I followed the procedure* ! Work is not a game. You should desperately try to understand the right action to take when confronted with a conundrum (I just learned that word and had to throw it in). Don't hide behind a procedure. Try to understand what is going on. Assigning blame can come later. How do I figure out what's the right thing to do?

I'm always suspicious of someone following *rules-of-thumb* or saying *we've always done it this way*. Times change. Economics change. New technology arrives. Innovations appear. Best practices get re-written.

Please do not use policies and procedures as a bludgeon to assign blame. They are intended to save your company time and money, not as tools to mete out punishment. It is very likely that someone not following a policy and procedure has found a flaw in their construction and this should lead to new and improved policies and procedures. Someone has thought about what they were doing instead of taking shelter behind a poor policy and procedure.

Some actual examples I have witnessed in my career:

Example 1: I was on a driving tour of a plant when I heard a loud, screeching sound, like a jet plane landing, but it went on and on and on. When I asked what the noise was, I was told that it was quite normal, nothing to be alarmed about, just high pressure steam being vented to the atmosphere by the boiler house. So I asked the next question, why were they venting high pressure steam? They replied that it was standard procedure when the steam demand went down to vent high pressure steam. So I asked the next question, why not produce less high pressure steam? I was told that they were following their standard procedure adopted many years before. I felt like I was questioning stone tablets. So I asked if anyone had looked at what it cost to buy raw water, purify the water, and then burn something to produce the steam, just to vent it? All I received were blank looks. Hey, I don't have to make this stuff up !

Example 2: I joined a small consulting company in 1985 that gathered data from individual petroleum refineries on every aspect of their operation, and then calculated several proprietary benchmarks or indicators to rate performance. No names or locations were ever disclosed and the company worked all over the world. If you had a refinery, you had heard of us, and we would come see you. A refinery could compare itself to geographic competitors and to size competitors, and look at performance gaps expressed as amounts of money.

My first task was to develop free market crude oil and product prices for each refinery in our studies. All went well until the study results were released to the clients. A refining vice-president at one of our clients disagreed with our crude oil prices as his data told him he was paying 50 cents per barrel more than our data showed. That was a lot of money, as he was responsible for several refineries. Our company president came into my office and jumped up and down on my desk (well, not literally, but it felt like it). I showed him all the data I had used, the public sources where I got the data, and reviewed all the spreadsheets I had developed. He understood it all and he went away. He came back an hour later, told me to pack up my files, and said we were getting on a plane the next morning to go see our client. The meeting was very cordial, our client could see where I had gotten the data, agreed with our calculations of prices at his refineries, but couldn't rationalize why his internal data showed higher prices than our prices. A few months went by, he called our president, and said he had solved the mystery.

Their crude oil buyer was a long term employee, well-known and well-liked in the industry. He liked to have all of the next month's crude oil purchases in place on the 25th day of the current month, and the whole industry knew it. On the 21st day of the month, quoted prices went up 10 cents per barrel, a small enough amount that it looked like noise in the statistical data and could be explained away in the market as uncertainty of Middle East politics, pending legislation in Washington, the latest economic data, or the phases of the moon. On the 22nd day of the month, it went up another dime, and so on until the 25th day of the month, when he set his crude purchases for the next month, and prices dropped 50 cents per barrel the next day. This guy had more fishing trips, hunting trips, golf outings, and fancy dinners for he and his wife than he could accept. But his procedure, and lack of analysis and internal auditing by the company, was costing his company millions of extra dollars every month.

EXAMPLE 3: I was visiting a refinery to review the data they had submitted for our study, when I noticed that they showed 172 people in the refinery laboratory, which was a very high number. It just leaped off the screen. I asked if it was true and was assured they had verified the data. During the refinery tour, I asked if we could stop by the laboratory. I counted about 40 heads which seemed about right for one shift. After dinner, I asked my host if he would mind stopping by the refinery and visiting the laboratory. He was very curious, but gracious, and I again counted about 40 heads, and it was a different shift. I explained my puzzlement and he admitted that the number was high because of all the sample bottles that had to be collected, analyzed, cleaned, and re-distributed to the operating units. So I then asked him about their sampling schedule. It turned out that when the refinery had started up over 40 years earlier, someone had decided that they needed to collect hourly samples of every crude oil that they processed and hourly samples of the feeds and products for each process unit. Their procedure hadn't changed in 40 years and no one had ever questioned it. I gently asked them if they had considered 24 hour composite samples, and whether they really needed all the sampling after operating the process units all these years. They agreed that they should look into it. The next set of data showed less than 20 people in the laboratory. I'm not patting myself on the back, but think about an outsider coming in and asking questions which you wouldn't think of asking because it had always been done that way.

EXAMPLE 4: The 2014 Winter Olympics were held in Sochi, Russia and the Olympic Committee was very concerned about the use of illegal performance-enhancing drugs. They commissioned a company to produce a tamper-proof sample bottle which was to be used to collect urine samples for every athlete in every event. They thought they had great procedures in place to catch any cheaters. The answer was really quite simple – the Russian teams figured out how to open the tamper-proof sample bottles and substitute *clean* samples. The sample bottles were not tamper-proof, nor were the procedures.

EXAMPLE 5: Once upon a time, a new bride cooked a roast for her new husband. He noticed that she cut about an inch off the end of the roast before putting it in the oven and asked her why she did that. Well, it was because her mother had always done that. Soon, the young couple had dinner at her parent's house, and her mother had also cut an inch off the end of the roast before putting it in the oven. You guessed it, her mother had done the same thing. Time passes and they all have dinner at grandma's house, and yes, she cooks a roast after cutting an inch off of it. When asked, grandma said her mother did it that way. Great-grandmother had passed on but grandma knew why she cut an inch off the roast – it wouldn't fit in her favorite roasting pan unless she cut off an inch. I'm glad she didn't do circumcisions.

Regardless of your business or profession, this story illustrates the folly of following long-time procedures without understanding the reasoning behind them. Just asking questions and discussing the reasoning behind established procedures can prove extremely valuable.

Remember the definition of insanity – doing the same thing over and over again and expecting a different result.

EXAMPLE 6: We've all seen pictures of the bleeding doctor being forcibly dragged off the airplane because the airline needed his seat for another passenger. It did not matter that the doctor had paid for the seat, or that he was scheduled to operate on several patients the following day in another city. What about the effects of his absence on his scheduled patients? Do they matter? Was the bureaucracy so rigid and punitive that *No One* was allowed to ask questions, or dare to use their brains, but encouraged to hide behind a written procedure, regardless of the circumstances? How many future passengers and future revenue was forever lost by the actions of that airline? Does every exception to a procedure need to be sent to the chairman of the board for a ruling? Absurd. Sounds like a German soldier in World War II.

EXAMPLE 7: I recently pulled into a service station to buy gasoline. It is a major US gasoline retailer with a convenience store, carwash, and a plethora of gas pumps. The little screen tells me to insert a grocery store card or a loyalty card – I had neither. I tried a VISA card - it wouldn't work. By now, I'm severely irritated. I lock the car, go inside the store, and tell the attendant that since this is a gas station – I'd like to buy gas – how do I do that? He also tells me to enter a grocery store card or a loyalty card, I have neither, and it won't take my VISA card. Now what? He tells me I can pre-pay with my VISA card (sigh of relief), how much do I want to buy? I told him I didn't know how much I wanted to buy as I wanted to fill up the tank. I finally guessed at a low number because I didn't want to stress him out by getting him to figure out how to do a credit. So here we have a major (big major) gasoline retailer with gas stations all over the country, driving away customers because of a procedure programmed into their system. I'll never buy gas from one of their stations again. And they won't miss me because I'm too small. Do they have a sales prevention team somewhere in their organization?

EXAMPLE 8: I go into a coffee shop regularly. You would recognize the name because they seem to be on every street corner. I ask for the largest cup of decaffeinated coffee they have because I can't drink caffeine. I'm told they don't make decaf after 1030AM. Why not, say I? It's a policy. Why do they have the policy? No one knows. I can't be the only customer in Dallas, TX that wants decaf. Now, I have a mission. The next day, I'm told 11AM. The next day, I'm told noon. I'm making progress, but I'm talking to different people. Could they be losing decaf sales because of a lack of supply? Wait, that's their business, isn't it?

EXAMPLE 9: I am visiting a refinery in the Middle East where I am proudly shown this enormous warehouse where they kept a spare for every piece of equipment in the refinery. When I asked why, they said that in the past, it took so long for deliveries to be made from manufacturers that it was more cost effective to have the spare equipment on hand, instead of being shut down and waiting. I gently suggested that with the proliferation of express delivery companies, they could probably get overnight delivery now and not have so much capital tied up in inventory. They were following an old procedure that had not been updated.

EXAMPLE 10: I roll my coins and take them to the bank to exchange for paper money. One day I took a roll of quarters (40 of them in a paper roll) to the drive-up window at the bank and asked for a $10 bill. The clerk asked to see my driver's license. I gave that to her. Then she asked if I had a debit card or a deposit slip. I gave her my debit card, but told her I didn't plan on making a deposit. I also asked her why she was asking for 2 forms of ID when I was just exchanging US coins for US currency – it was their policy – why did they have the policy – she didn't know and neither did the other people in the bank. Strange !

e. EVERY COMPANY NEEDS A JESUS

I'm not trying to be cute, funny, or irreverent but I think one of the great lessons of His life is that He got things done.

Every company, organization or any group of people working together to accomplish some common objectives desperately need one or more people who get things done. It's not enough to try or be diligent or to work hard – somebody has to get something done. You would like to have several people in your company emulating Jesus, but let me explain. Look at just some of the documented examples that Jesus gave us in his relatively short life here on Earth:

- Need water turned into wine – done.
- Need sick people healed – done.
- Need to catch fish – done.
- Need to feed a multitude – done.
- Need to calm a storm – done.
- Need to raise someone from the dead – done.
- Need someone to resist Satan's temptations – done.
- Need to die on the cross for our sins – done.

So what kind of people would populate your company if they followed the above examples?

- Show up for work every day
- Show up on time.
- Ask questions if they don't understand something
- Take time to think
- Solve problems when they arise
- Display a great sense of humor
- Don't take themselves so seriously
- Be kind towards each other
- Be willing to be teachers
- Demonstrate respect for each other
- Leave work on time – have a life.

What if your company doesn't have a Jesus in one particular, maybe over-looked area? Say that person is responsible for sending out invoices for work or services or products that have already been sent to the client or customer. But the company can't be paid for the above efforts because your company hasn't sent out invoices. Sounds simple, right? But the person whose job it is to send out invoices called in sick on Monday to recover from an exuberant weekend. That person also took a vacation day the following Friday to begin training for another long weekend. To compound the situation, the person who was supposed to approve the invoices being sent was out of the office, which delayed the whole process even further. Now the company has less money to pay its bills, may even be forced to lay off some people, and the whole situation was preventable.

Also look at the people who were supposed to receive the invoices that hadn't been sent. Their company is artificially flush with cash because their accounting system hasn't seen the invoices that haven't been sent and their recognized liabilities are lower than they should be. So they could make an ill-timed investment, thinking they had the cash because they hadn't taken into account the invoice they had not received. They should have anticipated it.

Now multiply this by the millions of companies in the world and you can easily imagine why every company needs people who copy Jesus – just get your job done.

f. STAGES OF A PROJECT

I don't care how large or small or complex or simple a project may be, you and many other team members will probably go through these 6 stages. Be ready to recognize them when they happen and don't get distracted by them:

1. *Enthusiasm* – everybody is fired up at first; something new and different to work on
2. *Disenchantment* – gee, maybe it doesn't look like as much fun as I thought it might be
3. *Panic* – how do I get out of this?
4. *Search for the Guilty* – who can we blame for this mess?
5. *Punishment of the Innocent* – let's pin it on someone else
6. *Decorations for Those Who Took No Part* – the few, the proud, the blameless

e. WHY IS THE TURTLE ON THE FENCEPOST?

It's a classic case of something that it couldn't do by itself – someone had to put it there. How often have you seen a person in a job that they were totally unsuited for and incapable of doing? It happens. And don't waste a second trying to understand it, other than realizing that someone put the turtle there. Eventually, the turtle will fall off the fencepost and the world will return to normal.

f. USE YOUR SENSES

The Army Rangers have an acronym when they are on patrol called *SLLS*, which stands for Stop, Look, Listen, and Smell, which simply told them to be aware of their surroundings, and pay attention to what their bodies were telling them. I didn't know about their method but used a similar system when I was visiting petroleum refineries. You can try out this system whenever you visit a new location, or even try it out in your own office:

- If I had a car, I would drive on the surrounding roads around the refinery.
- I would roll the window down to see what I could smell.
- I would listen to see what I could hear.
- I would look at the layout of the process units in the refinery.
- I would look for trash, rust, and piles of scrap equipment.
- I would look for steam leaks.
- I would look for groups of people standing around.
- I would look at the flares to see if they were burning.
- I would look for cranes to see if they were beginning, in the middle of, or just finished with a large maintenance effort, which meant the whole organization was probably stressed.
- I would show up in the lobby 30 minutes early and watch the people as they came into work: happy, frowning, smiling, quiet, telling jokes, grim, whatever I could detect.
- Then, when I met my contact at the appointed time, I knew a whole lot about the refinery before I had even talked to anyone. This approach proved to be very valuable, and it also gave me things to talk about.

i. WATCHING PEOPLE

It's very educational and very entertaining. I've been doing it my whole life. But do you really see? There is so much information out there but most of us aren't looking. We're so busy with our lives that we ignore what's happening around us.

You can surmise whole life stories just by watching people interact with each other and their families.

I have seen so many things, funny and humorous things, just by paying attention. It happens every day.

Especially pay attention to the people you're either buying from or selling to in your business. They're vitally important to your company. Go see them, talk to them, find out what makes them tick, what they need, what problems they have, how their problems may affect your business.

j. RANDALL MURPHY'S LAWS OF NEGOTIATION

Randall Murphy founded the Acclivus Corporation in Dallas, a consultancy that worries about relationships, not only within companies but between companies. He developed 10 guidelines for developing long-lasting relationships that increase sales/profits and that are good for both sides as listed in an article in the Dallas Morning News in 1975:

1. One deal does not a relationship make. Take a long-term view.
2. Power in negotiation is insight. Figure out what the other guy really needs, which may not be what's being demanded.
3. Ask questions that will lead you to solutions for the client.

4. Differentiate your products or services by adding value to the customer – not by cutting prices.

5. Maintain parity in negotiations so that both sides come out winners. If you reduce your price, get a concession in return, say, a longer length of contract.

6. Convey careful consideration. Concessions that seem arbitrary or knee-jerk invite additional demands and create skepticism. Conversely, provide a strong rationale versus a weak excuse when turning down a demand.

7. Do not undercut your staff and try to save the day by cutting a deal. It destroys trust and weakens future dealings.

8. Involve those on the other side in diagnosing the problem, so that they are committed to the proposed solution.

9. Don't be held hostage by your timetable or be rushed by theirs. There are more screw-ups in well-intended negotiations brought on by deadline pressures.

10. Don't jump the gun in creating a contract. Find fundamental agreement first.

XI

BOSSES

a. HOW TO WORK WITH YOUR BOSS

When you go to work, you need to think about and understand where you fit in the organizational structure and how the group that you are a part of fits in the organization:

- What role does your group play?
- What need are you filling?
- What parts of the organization look to your group for support?
- What tasks does your group perform for other groups?

Most organizations are structured similar to the military:

- Privates report to corporals
- Corporals report to sergeants
- Sergeants report to...well, you get the idea.

Somewhere in this maze sits your boss. You will look to your boss for work assignments, guidance, feedback, wisdom, and opinions. Your boss is not perfect or omnipotent. But you *must* respect your boss. I have worked for some bosses who were so bad that I wondered how they found their way to work in the morning. I was also fortunate to work for some talented and brilliant leaders.

- The boss is the boss !
- The 2nd most important person in your life, if you're married
- Do not approach your job passively by waiting for your boss to give you something to do.
- You are not a piece of furniture.
- Ask your boss how you can help and you will never be idle again.
- Be proactive – never passive.

Let's imagine your boss is sitting in his office with problems stacked all over the desk, problems stacked on shelves, problems stacked all over the floor, etc. In walks employee A who proudly says, "Boss, I've found a problem !" The boss thinks to himself, "★★★★★ ! Just what I needed !" Alternatively, employee B walks in and says, "Boss, I've found a problem, I've evaluated the problem, I think I have found three potential solutions to the problem, and I'd like to hear your opinion on the best solution we should implement to solve the problem."

- Which one, A or B, will the boss like to see walking into his office?
- Which one, A or B, will the boss be more likely to give a promotion?
- Don't *ever* just take problems to your boss – take solutions.
- Effort and analysis trumps laziness every time.

- You make your own luck – it's called perseverance meets opportunity.
- Study your boss – likes, dislikes, actions, behavior, habits, pet peeves, raw nerves.
- Find out what information the boss needs to do their job.
- Find out where your boss goes to get the information they need.
- Find out how your boss analyzes the information and makes an action plan.
- Find out if there are other sources of information your boss may not know about.
- Ask your boss how decisions are made – understand the thought process.
- Be at your desk before your boss gets to work.
- Understand the job below you in the organization perfectly.
- Strive to understand your job perfectly.
- Don't be afraid to re-define your job and stretch your limits.
- Study your bosses like they are your 8th grade science fair project.

b. WHAT DOES A GOOD BOSS LOOK LIKE?

I've had a few, learned to treasure them, and they all had similar characteristics:

- Door is always open
- Give assignments and leave you alone until you think you're finished
- Answer questions and make suggestions when your ship runs aground
- Brutally honest with you

- Allow you freedom to follow your ideas to conclusion
- Don't want to re-write what you have written – how will you learn, otherwise
- Sink or swim, it's up to you
- Back you up with everyone, up to and including the Big Boss
- Let's you fail and suggests how to learn from it
- Can see right through any BS – vicious eyesight

Bill Parcells was a long-time successful football coach, his teams won Super Bowls, he's in the Pro Football Hall of Fame, and he was universally loved by his players for one simple reason: he was brutally honest with them. No beating around the bush. No consideration for their feelings. He was color-blind, blunt, and very successful. If they asked a question, he answered it using small words with several profanities mixed in so they clearly understood what he was saying. If they made mistakes, he would tell them. If they played poorly, he would tell them. If they asked what they should be doing differently, he would tell them. He didn't wait for them to ask questions, he always told them what they needed to hear, not what they wanted to hear. Guys would run through walls for him.

Care and Feeding of a "Good Boss":

- Cherish them
- Worship the ground they walk on
- Treat it as a great learning opportunity
- Be brutally honest with them but be nice about it
- Learn and practice tact
- Don't keep any secrets from them – you don't know what they might need to know
- Learn how and when to approach them

- Always remember that they're human too
- Learn their hot buttons and never push one
- Keep them informed about things you think they ought to know
- Beat their butts at golf and gin rummy – they won't respect you if you roll over and let them win. They are very competitive or they wouldn't have the job they have.
- Don't spread gossip.

Be grateful for a few good mentors that appear in your life. You won't truly appreciate how lucky you are until they're no longer in your life. They are precious gifts to be handled with care and given the greatest respect. Their influences on you will be deep and long-lasting. They were put in your life for a reason.

I worked for one company where the president kept around a vice-president who didn't really have much responsibility. We finally figured out that he was the company SOB, the one person in a group of yes-men who would always tell the president the truth, regardless of whether the president wanted to hear it or not. It's a valuable role, and the president was honest enough to realize that he needed that person in that role.

The same is true for enemies and pains-in-the-butt. I had to clean up that language a lot, but you will also have some of the opposite species. They are also put in your life for reasons you may not comprehend at the time. You may not like it, you don't have to like it, but you can still learn from them. It's a different kind of gift but still a teaching moment.

c. HOW TO WORK FOR A "BAD" BOSS

I've had a few. I remember one boss who was so introverted that I had to stand in the hall and spread my arms out to get him to say "Good Morning" back to me. He wouldn't talk – left me notes whenever I was out of my office.

I had another boss who wanted status reports on all of my projects at 8AM, Noon, and 5PM.

I had another boss who took credit for anything positive that happened and blamed me for everything negative that happened. He and his boss carpooled every day. DUH.

I had another boss who forbid me from ever talking to his boss.

Let's speculate (this is fun) about why these people acted the way they did:

- Insecure
- Poor self image
- Ignorant
- Inexperience
- Fear
- Out of comfort zone as a boss
- Disorganized
- Unclear work plan
- Unclear objectives
- Jealousy
- Untrained
- Poor communicator
- Beats you down to feel better about themselves
- Control freak

- Unable to give a compliment
- Wouldn't recognize a good idea if tripped over it
- They are still human beings.
- The pointy-haired boss in Dilbert is alive and well !

All of the above points are in play but do not absolve you from thinking about how to work with your *bad* boss.

What to do?

- You could get another job – may not be an ideal solution but it is one answer.
- You can stand on your head for awhile. A company can be like a circus – things are always moving around and changing so stick it out for awhile.
- Study your *bad* boss like they are your 8th grade science fair project. It's still a teaching moment.
- What makes the *bad* boss tick?
- Why do you think the boss is *bad*?
- Can the *bad* boss be house-broken and potty-trained?
- What are the strengths and weaknesses of the *bad* boss?
- How can you help the *bad* boss?
- How does the *bad* boss think?
- *Never* make an end run around the *bad* boss. They will eventually hang themselves because if it's obvious to you, it will be obvious to a lot of other people, too. And the *bad* boss may still have enough influence to hurt you badly if you try that tactic.

There is an old story of the Arab sheik that caught a peasant boy with his young and beautiful daughter. He threatened to kill the peasant boy, but the peasant boy offered the sheik a deal. "Do you see your beautiful stallion over there in the pasture?

If you will spare my life for one year, I will teach your horse to fly!" The friends of the peasant boy thought he was crazy. He said, "In a year's time the sheik might die, I might die, or who knows, maybe I can teach the horse to fly, but I've gained a year."

Notice that there are similarities in how you treat a *good* boss and how you treat a *bad* boss.

d. HEAVEN IN AN ORGANIZATION

A good friend of mine told me about a petrochemical plant in South Texas at which he had worked and which turned out to be the best job he had ever had. A new plant manager arrived and called a meeting for all of his direct reports and all of the people who worked for them. He introduced himself, had a distinguished presence, tall, erect, white-haired, smiling, and said, "Even as we are talking, some maintenance workers are taking away the door to my office. I don't have an open-door policy, I have a no-door policy. Furthermore, I'm going to tell all of you how we are going to run this plant. I'm not going to make any decisions. I'm totally uninterested in how many rolls of toilet paper we will need this week. That's a decision one of you will make because I won't make that decision or any other decision. All of you will be making the decisions on how this plant will be run. I intend to push the decision-making as far down in the organization as I can – that is my primary job. Once anyone did make a decision, they and everyone else would have to live with it. I expect some bad decisions will be made – that's part of the learning process. You may come to me at any time with questions, ask for advice or counsel, or to discuss any situation, but I refuse to go anywhere that smells like, walks like, or sounds like a decision. If anyone develops a history of making bad decisions, we will find someone else to make decisions."

One immediate effect of this principle was an immediate improvement in communications. No one wanted to make a bad decision, so everyone talked to a great many people, gathered facts, sought opinions, looked for problem areas, tried to discover what you didn't know, before making decisions, so that you could make the best decision possible.

Some people, either bravely or foolishly, approached the new plant manager with situations, and tried to manipulate decision making. They could be seen coming from a mile away, and the plant manager steadfastly refused to fall into those traps. They were shot down in flames, and word of their fiery descents spread through the plant grapevine at the speed of light.

Everyone was also empowered to ask questions of anyone else at any time. If you don't understand something, speak up. You would be frowned at for not asking questions.

The plant manager also became famous for daily walks throughout the plant, at any hour and on any day, to find out what was going on, what were the concerns, what were the problems? Since there was no isolation in an office making all of those weighty decisions, the plant manager was free to wander.

My friend said it took a couple of months before everyone bought into the program, indeed, it was about all they talked about, 24/7.

When the plant manager finally retired, at the biggest retirement party anyone remembered, the main street through the plant was renamed, to help everyone recall and educate new employees about the lessons they had learned.

MBWA – management by wandering around – what a concept.

e. CONDITIONAL RESPECT

In the early days of computer programming language, we would use a lot of *IF* statements. If a number was within a certain range, you would take a specific action. If a number exceeded a certain value, you would take a different action. If a number was below a certain value, you would take another action.

If you practice conditional respect with your co-workers, or even with your boss, they can never win, in your eyes. It's a flawed concept to start with. As soon as they satisfy some unknown criteria that you have set for them, you'll just set some new unknown conditions that, in your judgment, they will now have to meet. This is a very selfish and dangerous game for you to play and the other folks are going to figure out what you're doing very quickly, with bad news headed your way.

The philosophical opposite of the above is unconditional love between spouses. Regardless of what your spouse says or does, the other spouse will still love them.

Conditional love between spouses doesn't work because the actions in paragraph 2 above will take place.

Unconditional respect for your boss and co-workers implies some key principles that you must practice consistently:

1. Always be honest.
2. Trust your co-workers to give you the same respect you give them.
3. Be a teacher. When you see the opportunity for a teaching moment, just do it, tactfully.
4. Spend more time listening than talking. The words *silent* and *listen* contain the same letters of the alphabet, just arranged differently.
5. You can't learn anything with your mouth open.
6. Be careful with secrets. If you're told or learn something in confidence, always respect that confidence. Don't ever say, "Oh yeah, I already knew that." That's just your ego talking.
7. Look for diamonds in the rough. You never know where you will find them.
8. Always watch other people very carefully. I treat interactions like I'm playing a card game such as bridge or poker. There are *tells* that everyone has that are free information for you: facial expressions, gestures, posture, body language, and eyes. We all do it. Pay attention !
9. Listen to people very carefully. Their choice of words and how they use them in sentences also give you free information. They might disclose things you didn't know or weren't supposed to know, so be discrete.
10. Pay attention to their grammar. Whenever I hear poor grammar, I subconsciously suspect what they're saying because I suspect the logic of their thought process and how well organized their thought process is to get

to that point. But I still listen ! What they are saying is not negated by my biases. Just because they can't express themselves very well doesn't mean that it's not the greatest thing since banana splits and root beer floats ! *Listen* ! How hard can it be?

11. I'm also suspicious of people who use a great deal of profanity. I'm not a prude, but I wonder if their vocabulary is so small that their goal is to use the F word as a noun, verb, adjective, and adverb in the same sentence. That's not communication – it's playgrounds and high school football. Come on, man. I'm sure you can talk without using the Lord's name in vain in every sentence if you'd just try. I've let a few choice words slip out when the car beside me cuts me off. "Was the written part of the test for your driver's license optional or just the driving part?" My wife has worked very hard to get me to stop using hand and finger signals to educate other drivers. I now imagine every other driver with a loaded .45 on the seat beside them.

f. GO OUT & MAKE MISTAKES

Once upon a time, I had a boss who told me to go out and make mistakes. This is *not* a fairy tale. I of course objected because I had gone to the school of thought where mistakes were leapt upon with much verbal abuse and poor appraisals. He told me that he didn't work that way. He was giving me his verbal approval and blanket permission to screw things up. I was naturally suspicious. He told me that his primary job in the company was to get promotions for all the people that reported to him. And if he couldn't get that done, the failure was on him.

When I got up off of the floor, he explained a very simple equation to me: the only way I was going to get promoted was to learn to make good decisions; the only way I was going to learn to make good decisions was to make some bad decisions (and I would go on to make some doozies). "Don't be afraid to make some mistakes – I expect you to do that. And I will always ask you what you learned. Try and fail and try again."

Life is like a basketball game (you thought I was going to say a box of chocolates?). You don't win the game by only making one shot. You don't lose the game by making a single mistake on defense. Win/loss records mean nothing. Tall players versus short players mean nothing. It's really the summation of a whole series of events, by both sides, and the winner is *always* the team that scores the most points – that's why you keep score. It's how well each side played the game, that day, under those conditions. Period.

There are no shortcuts to learning how to make good decisions. It's called getting *experience* and it can be a frustrating and painful process. You learn very little from your successes – just affirmation of logical thinking and analysis. You will learn so much more from analyzing your failures. Treat it like a crime scene with CSI's Grissom by your side:

- First thing, what do you see? Don't just look, really observe.
- What don't you see?
- What could it all mean?
- What doesn't make sense?
- How could it have happened?
- What do you know for dead certain sure?
- What don't you know?

- Is there an alternative story that fits the facts?
- How do we go about getting more information?
- What are the effects of the mistakes you have made?
- How do you get help from whom to figure all this out?
- Could you have done something differently to get a better outcome?

Realize that it's up to you to figure all this out ! All kinds of generally well-meaning people will be absolutely thrilled to help point out how badly you messed up and what you should have said and done differently. But listen to them ! There may be a pony in there somewhere. There may be a diamond hidden in all that rhetoric and noise.

There's a great line in Marvin Gaye's recording of *Heard It Through the Grapevine*: "Believe half of what you see and none of what you hear." There aren't any, or at least very few absolutes in this world. Beware of the words *always* and *never* – they have teeth and can rise up and bite you in the butt.

g. DECISION MAKING

This is going to sound very similar to the section on "Problem Solving", but with one significant difference – now you have to do something. Once you have finally defined the problem and figured out a solution, what do you now do? A lot of people will wait, think they need more information, need to talk to a few more folks, sleep on it, mull it over for a while, meditate, get another cup of coffee, etc.

My favorite former *boss* had some simple rules and a simple motto:

- When you think you have about 75% of the information you need to make a decision, go ahead. You will *never* have 100% of what you think you need to know to make your decision.
- *Get the big decisions right* – don't sweat the small stuff.
- *Be confident* – you're right until proven wrong.
- *Take a position and defend it* – an old lawyer's maxim
- *When all is said and done, more will be said than done.*
- *If someone says they're not trying to throw you under the bus, they probably are.*
- *If a politician's lips are moving, they're lying.*
- *Things can be destroyed much quicker than they're built.*
- *No one said it was going to be a fair fight.*
- *You can step on your ★★★★, just don't stand on it.*
- *If you're in a hole, stop digging !*

MOTTO: You can always find an excuse to wait !

His reasoning also was that you need to develop your *gut instinct*, that inner voice that tells you what to do. Of course, you can still screw things up, but that is the yellow brick road called *experience* and you earn it the hard way.

Ronald Reagan to the graduating class at the Naval Academy on 22 May 1985: "Your countrymen have faith in you and expect you to make decisions. The issues will not be black-and-white; otherwise there would be no decision to make. Do not be afraid to admit and consider your doubts, but don't be paralyzed by them. Be brave. Make your judgment and then move forward with confidence, knowing that although there's never 100% certainty, you have chosen what you believe to be the right course. Do this, and the American people will always back you up."

If decision making was easy, Charlie McCarthy could do it. If you don't know Charlie McCarthy, look up Candace Bergen's father, Edgar.

You have to break a few eggs to make an omelet.

h. 10 COMMANDMENTS OF BUSINESS FAILURE

It's a book by Donald Keough (Portfolio, 2011), past president of the Coca-Cola Company, which clearly states the actions that a business should never take:

1. *Quit Taking Risks* – when you stop thinking that things could be better, you're in trouble. When you think you're a near monopoly and that you're approaching invulnerability, you're vulnerable. Why do cars still have glove compartments?
2. *Be Inflexible* – If you don't build a better mousetrap, someone else will. If you're the immovable object and you meet the irresistible force, you're going to break.
3. *Isolate Yourself* – ignore your customers, your clients, and your own employees. Total buy-in to your self-proclaimed, mythic, god-like status, and look for a soft landing spot for the inevitable fall.
4. *Assume Infallibility* – You can play *The Blame Game* to avoid any sense of responsibility. Read the book !
5. *Play Close to the Foul Line* – customers, investors, and employees have put their trust in management. Fail them and you fail yourself. Trying to skirt the edges of barely avoiding the trifecta of dishonest, unethical, and immoral is not a business plan.

6. *Fail to Take Time to Think* - Just because it can be done doesn't mean it should be done. Have you thought it all the way through? Pros and cons? Plans B, C, D, E, F, etc.

7. *Put All Your Faith in Experts and Outside Consultants* – who anointed these paid supplicants to place gentle kisses on various sensitive portions of your anatomy? Do you have any faith that they won't just tell you exactly what you want to hear? And you paid for the castle/moat to protect yourself from any criticism, both inside and outside your castle walls? Just where were the outside directors hiding when Enron crashed and burned?

8. *Love Your Bureaucracy* – companies ruled by procedures waste time dotting i's and crossing t's. We were just following the rules ! Although we don't know the reasons, the logic, or the economic reasons that led to the original creation of the rules. Did everyone lock their brains in the trunks of their cars when they left home?

9. *Send Mixed Signals* – nothing spells confusion like flying first class and telling all your employees to fly coach. Different strokes for different folks? No, just inconsistent definition and follow-through on lousy policy and procedures. Do I smell a whiff of entitlement?

10. *Fear the Future* – if you buy into doom and gloom, you'll get what you pay for. Placing your head neck-deep in your anatomy or in a pile of sand is not a mission statement nor an action plan for your business.

XII

PROBLEM SOLVING 101

a. HOW TO SOLVE PROBLEMS

One Saturday morning, I got the lawnmower out of the garage for the weekly suburban ritual of the mowing of the grass. Regardless of how many times I pulled the starter cord, the mower just sat there defiantly glaring at me. I kicked it. I cursed it. The air turned blue. I pulled the sparkplug out and cleaned it. I pulled the starter cord a few more times. Finally, I looked in the gas tank and saw that it was empty.

Unfortunately, this is the approach many of use to go about solving problems. We stagger, stumble, and trip like a one-legged blind person learning to square dance. Never fear, I am going to teach you how to go about solving problems. But first, one of my favorite stories.

After World War II in Japan, a man named Sedichi Toyoda ran a small manufacturing plant that made small figurines that were sold in shops and used as decorative items in homes all over the country. Knick-knacks like a small cat that was sitting on its hind feet and licking one of its front paws. The cats were cast in clay, fired in a kiln, and then painted. On this particular day, the cats were coming out of the casting machine minus their right ear. There was a pile of earless cats in the trash when Mr. Toyoda arrived, jumped onto a table, and shouted *Stop* at the top of his lungs. Since he was the boss, everybody stopped what they were doing and gathered around him:

1. *WHY* are the cats that are coming out of the casting machine missing their right ears? After much conversation, the consensus answer was that the machine operator didn't know how to operate the machine.
2. *WHY* doesn't the machine operator know how to operate the machine? Consensus answer, "It's a new machine and the operator has never received any training."
3. *WHY* hasn't the operator received any training to know how to operate the new machine? Consensus answer, "No one has called the manufacturer to ask them about training."
4. *WHY* hasn't anyone called the manufacturer to see if they offer training? Consensus answer, "No one has been assigned to call the manufacturer to see if they offer training for the new machine."?
5. *WHY* doesn't someone call the manufacturer and get someone out here to train the operator on the new machine?

This may be a simplistic example, but Mr. Toyoda believed that any problem could be solved if you asked *WHY* 5 times. Think it might work for you? Mr. Toyoda was one of many astute business people who rebuilt Japan after World War II and went on to start many successful businesses. One of them was a car company named after him with one letter changed in his last name.

Another example:

1. *WHY* is my child getting poor math grades in school? They're bored.
2. *WHY* are they bored? They've not been challenged in class.
3. *WHY* aren't they being challenged in class? The teacher isn't very good. Yeah, blame the coach.
4. *WHY* isn't the teacher any good? The teacher is using the standard material for that class.
5. *WHY* isn't the child in an advanced placement class? Gee, why didn't we think of that?

Everyone thinks they know how to solve problems, but have you ever thought about the process of solving a problem? Or are you like the blind, one-legged man above?

Try this approach:

1. What do you think is the problem?
   > Can you write down the problem using simple words?
   > Is it really the problem or are you dealing with a symptom?
   > You can't solve a symptom.
   > Keep asking yourself "what is the problem?"

   > You can't accomplish anything until you finish step # 1.

105

2. Do *not* leap towards the first answer that tumbles through your tiny brain.

> There are no blue ribbons awarded for speed.
>
> Actually, speed slows down success in problem solving.
>
> Depend on it, your first instinct is often wrong.

3. Think hard. I know it's tough to do.

> What true facts do you know indisputably to be true?
>
> Do you know the facts that you don't know?
>
> Can you find out the facts that you don't know?
>
> Trying to solve a problem when you don't know all the facts can be impossible, embarrassing, costly, and/or dangerous.

4. What are all the possible solutions to the problem?

> No limits.
>
> Blue sky solutions are OK.
>
> Be silly.
>
> Write down all the possible answers you can think of.

5. Now the hardest part:

> How can you figure out the best solution to the problem?
>
> For my lawnmower, putting gasoline in the tank was an obvious answer.
>
> Most problems may not have such a simple solution.

Are their practical constraints to your possible solutions?

Are their knowledge constraints to your possible solutions?

Are their financial constraints to your possible solutions?

Was your problem statement too ambitious?

Was your problem statement too vague?

Is your best solution practically feasible?

Many times I have made a list using 2 columns, pro and con. Does that help?

Think the problem and your solution all the way through. It's like a chess game – you need to think several moves ahead. – don't stop part way.

6. Go for it! Thomas Edison said he had failed 10,000 times for every success that he had had. That sounds like hyperbole but you get the point.

7. If you fail, go back to step 1. Many times, the mis-statement of the problem proves to be your undoing.

8. Try re-writing the problem statement using different nouns and verbs. It's surprising how often this can break a mental log jam.

9. Now for the really fun part: See if you can use this solution on other problems – the whole process may happen much quicker.

b. STORIES ABOUT PROBLEM SOLVING – EACH WITH A LESSON

I best learn about life by listening to stories. Being an unrepentant sports nut, many of my stories are about sports, but they all have a point. All of these stories are about solving problems. There is a lesson or a point or a moral buried somewhere in each story.

Abe Lemons was a long time, very successful basketball coach at the University of Texas. But when he first got out of college, the only job he could find was as a track and field coach at a small high school. Now Abe didn't know a damned thing about track and field, so he had a problem, and he set about solving it. He assembled everyone who had come out for the track and field team at the starting line of the quarter mile oval track and said, "When I shoot off this starting pistol, I want all of you to run as fast as you can, keep turning left, get back here as quick as you can, and keep running around this track until you can't run no more." He then went to the opposite side of the track, and shot off his pistol:

- The first small group of boys to the 100 yard mark would run the 100 yard dash
- The first small group of boys to the 220 yard mark would run the 220 yard dash
- The first small group of boys to get back to the starting line would run the 440 yard dash
- The first small group of boys to run around the track twice would run the 880
- The first small group of boys to run around the track 4 times would run the mile
- Abe recruited the quarterback from the football team to throw the javelin
- Abe recruited two tackles from the football team to throw the discus and shot put
- Abe recruited two forwards from the basketball team to high jump and long jump
- Voila ! Abe had a track and field team.

When Steve Jobs was shown the first model of the iPhone, he dropped it on the floor, and watched it break apart. He then took out his car keys, scratched up the glass surface of the phone, and said to his development team, "You need to fix these 2 problems."

When Steve Kerr joined the Chicago Bulls pro basketball team, Michael Jordan didn't know if he could trust this unproven rookie in crunch time when the game was on the line. His solution was to pick a fight with Steve in practice one day – if Steve wasn't willing to fight him, Michael didn't feel like he could trust him. They fought, and later that year, Michael passed Steve the ball for the shot that won the Bulls an NBA championship.

McDonalds spends a lot of time and money researching new restaurant sites, analyzing traffic patterns, population densities, demographics, and proximity to schools before building on a new site. Burger King watches where McDonalds builds a new restaurant and puts one of their restaurants on the opposite street corner.

Willie Mays was a 5 tool major league baseball player and maybe the best and most complete player to ever play the game: hit for high average, hit with power, run, field, and throw. But what Willie really loved to do was win. He didn't care about his statistics and told the sportswriters that they could keep track of them, he wasn't interested. He was discussing triples (a relatively rare hit in baseball) with a sportswriter one day and said, "If I hit a long drive and am not certain I can make it safely all the way to 3rd base, I'll stop at 1st base." The sportswriter asked Willie why he wouldn't at least go on to 2nd base. Willie said, "If I go to 2nd base, Willie McCovey is batting behind me and he won't see anything good to hit, just a bunch of slow curveballs and changeups. But if I'm on 1st base and a threat to steal 2nd base, Willie will see lots of fastballs, and Willie is a good, good fastball hitter. The sportswriter asked him what happens if McCovey makes an out? Willie said, "Well, I can always steal 2nd base !" Willie Mays had a problem, thought strategically, and found the best solution for his team.

Personal note: I was once in the centerfield bleachers at Crosley Field in Cincinnati and saw Willie McCovey hit a baseball over the centerfield scoreboard, easily a 500 foot home run.

Willie Nelson was being interviewed for his biography and asked his biographer if he knew about the rules for Willie's tour bus? The biographer laughed and said, "I didn't know you had any rules !" Willie said he didn't care what anyone smoked or drank, but he had 2 inviolate rules that everyone had to follow.

RULE 1: *No Drugs!* If Willie caught anyone with drugs, he would stop the bus and kick their butts off in the middle of nowhere. "People have paid good money to see our shows, and anyone on drugs can't play their instruments, can't remember the words to the songs, and you're worthless to the band." The biographer asked if anyone had ever tested Rule 1 and Willie said that people can be pretty stupid and there were probably some people out there somewhere who were still trying to hitchhike home.

RULE 2: The bus stops at 8:00AM every morning, lets Willie off, and drives ahead 6 miles. Willie said, "When I was younger, I would jog the 6 miles to the bus, then I started walking, now I ride my bicycle. But the bus stops at 8:00AM every morning.

Don Drysdale was a pitcher for the Los Angeles Dodgers and was not having a good day – not a happy camper. Runners on 2nd and 3rd base, one out, and their manager, Walter Alston, walks out to the mound. "Don, let's walk this batter, load the bases, get a double play, and get out of the inning." Alston was barely back in the dugout when he hears a cry of pain and looks back to see the batter trotting down to 1st base rubbing his ribs where Drysdale's fastball had hit him. Alston shouted out, "Why did you hit him?" Drysdale answered, "You wanted him on 1st base, didn't you?" What Drysdale did actually makes a lot of sense:

- He threw 1 pitch instead of 4 pitches to walk the batter
- He eliminated any risk of a ball not being caught in throwing 4 pitches
- The ball was dead and all action stopped as soon as it hit the batter – automatic timeout
- The runners on 2nd and 3rd base couldn't move.

Alberto Lombardi immigrated from Italy to Dallas, TX and began his career washing dishes. He saved his money and opened *Lombardi's* which was an instant success, and he now owns 17 restaurants around the country. He has loaned money to his 3 daughters to open their own restaurants, which they have repaid with interest. He only has one business rule: no employee ever shows disrespect to each other, or to a supplier, or to a customer. If anyone does that, they are fired on the spot. He thinks that disrespect is a cancer, eating away at the businesses he has created, and he simply won't tolerate it.

Baker Mayfield was not recruited after a very successful high school career as a quarterback in Austin, TX, although he had always dreamed of playing major college football. So he decided to walk on at Texas Tech University without a football scholarship. He started and won the first 5 games as a freshman and got hurt. When he recovered, he did not get his starting job back, and was not offered a scholarship. So he left and walked on at the University of Oklahoma, soon earning a scholarship, where he started and won for the next 3 years. As a senior, he won the Heisman trophy as the best college football player in the country. He is the only walk-on to ever win the Heisman trophy. Then the Cleveland Browns made him the 1st pick in the 1st round of the NFL draft. He never gave up !

A company built a new crude oil distillation tower at their refinery and it wouldn't work. A distillation tower simply depends on contact between heated vapor and liquid to separate into specific components ranging from very light to very heavy products, and this tower just would not perform. All the company experts came in. The tower was inspected from top to bottom and nothing was found that would keep it from working. There were so many people in the control room that they could have put in bleachers. Following the definition of insanity, they started up the tower again and got the same results. Heads were vigorously scratched. Then, a rookie civil engineer who had just started working at the refinery, and knew nothing about distillation, walked into the control room and asked why the tower was leaning 5 degrees to the east? Everyone took turns laughing at him, and they told him he was crazy because the tower had just been erected and was brand new. He calmly said he had 2 sextants outside on intersecting roads and they could come see for themselves. The tower needs to be vertical so that the trays are level and you can get good contact between the vapor and liquid, which wasn't happening because the tower was leaning. He was right and they had to begin a massive project to return the tower to its intended vertical position when it worked just as designed. The last time I was at that refinery, that brash rookie civil engineer had become the refinery manager, because he had found the solution to a problem.

Gregg Popovich is the long time and very successful head coach of the San Antonio Spurs in the National Basketball Association. He is hard on his players and they universally love him. He has never taken any credit for their success in winning 5 NBA championships. "I never played a single minute or scored a single point in any game," he said after his 1,000th victory. At one point, he had a French point guard, an Argentine shooting guard, a Virgin Islands center, and several players from Africa and Europe on his team. "When I got out of their way and let them just play, they became much better basketball players."

Jay Leno always impressed me because he vowed at the start of his comedy career never to use a single profane word. He believed that using profanity was just a way to get a cheap laugh, because people would laugh, even if what was said wasn't funny. Remember that he started out as a stand-up comic working 250 nights a year before his long-time stint as the host of the *Tonight Show*. Stand-up comedy was where he practiced and perfected his craft, and he still does it today because he loves it. Jay vowed that he was going to be funny without resorting to getting cheap laughs because of profanity and he's still doing it. He solved the problem of being funny his way.

Dick Williams was the manager of the Oakland Athletics in a World Series game against the Cincinnati Reds. Two outs, runners on 2nd and 3rd base, tie game, Johnny Bench at bat, 3 balls and 2 strikes, and Dick calls time out. Catfish Hunter was pitching for Oakland and Dick tells Catfish to ignore all of his hand motions of pointing to Bench, pointing to 1ˢᵗ base, holding up 4 fingers to indicate he wanted Catfish to walk Bench, and told him to throw the pitch right over the middle of the plate. Johnny Bench stood there with his bat on his shoulder and watched strike 3. Dick had solved his problem with theatrics and trickery.

Sherlock Holmes had a case called *The Dog That Didn't Bark*. He had been called to a house where the wife had been murdered and a small dog was standing there barking at him. "Is this dog always here?" Yes. "Does he always bark?" Only at strangers. "Arrest the husband for the murder."

A sportswriter was watching Jack Nicklaus on the practice range and he noticed that Jack never took his eyes off his golf ball until it had hit the ground and stopped rolling. He said to Jack, "It's almost as if you can stare down the golf ball and make it go exactly where you want it to go." Jack replied, "Oh, I can."

I was playing bridge at lunch several years ago when one of the players was missing the queen of trumps. He had the ace of trumps in his hand and the king of trumps in the dummy and could finesse either way. Seems like an insoluble problem or simply a guess, right? This player found a 100% guaranteed way to succeed. You get a bonus of 100 points in rubber bridge if you hold 4 of the 5 top cards in the trump suit in one hand. This is commonly referred to as *100 honors*. Our hero calmly declared a 100 honors, and the person holding the queen said, "No, you don't" to great merriment. Now the way to finesse for the queen was known. It was the perfect trifecta of being simultaneously illegal, unethical, and immoral, but he had found a solution to a problem that would have been at best a guess. We threw the hand in and didn't play it, but I was jealous. What great thinking ! How many of us, when faced with a difficult problem, aren't creative enough to think of unique solutions. I'm not advocating cheating, just thinking.

Willie Stargell was a great power-hitting first baseman for the Pittsburgh Pirates and was playing in the All-Star game in the Houston Astrodome. He reached 1st base and either mis-read a sign, it was a full moon, or he just decided to take off for 2nd base. It really wasn't an attempted steal as you didn't use a stopwatch to measure Willie's foot speed – a calendar would have been more appropriate. He was going to be out by the proverbial country mile. So he's chugging along, the 2nd baseman is standing on 2nd base counting the 108 stitches in the baseball, everyone is smiling, and Willie goes into a slide about 15 feet from the base, pops up, and turns to the umpire to call timeout. When everyone stopped laughing, Willie was tagged out, and returned to the dugout. Hey, I didn't say it was a great solution to Willie's problem, but it makes a good story.

I play duplicate bridge with a retired psychologist who worked for a major airline. Of course, I asked what he did at the airline and he said he tried to mediate disputes and arguments before they turned into grievances, arbitrations, or lawsuits. Then he told me an interesting story about Herb Kelleher, who at the time was president of Southwest Airlines (a chapter on Herb appears later). A small airline on the East Coast was using an advertising slogan that Southwest had been using. At his airline, they would have just called the legal department and told them to sue the bastards. Not Herb. He called the president of the small airline and told him that Southwest wasn't going to sue him, but that Herb would arm-wrestle him for the right to the advertising slogan. Of course, Herb had publicity shots taken of him chain-smoking in his office and doing arm curls using a fifth of Wild Turkey bourbon. Herb rented Reunion Arena, had a boxing ring installed, and flew the president of the small airline to Dallas for the showdown. Herb comes out in boxing gloves, boxing trunks, robe, smoking a cigarette, and somehow holding up a glass of Wild Turkey. I don't know who *won* the match but Southwest Airlines got a ton of free publicity for the stunt. A different kind of solution to a problem.

Doug Harvey was a long-time major league baseball umpire. His first major league series in which he was an umpire was in St. Louis and he said that was where he learned why everyone called Stan Musial *Stan the Man*. Doug was behind home plate for the first time in the third game of the series and Stan was batting. Bases loaded, 2 outs, a count of 3 balls and 2 strikes, when the next pitch came towards the edge of home plate. Doug raised his right arm, signifying strike 3, and the ball broke to the right and missed home plate by a good 4 inches. Doug had a problem, he had already made the call, it was a really bad call, and he couldn't correct it. So there he was, with egg all over his face, in his first game behind home plate, and everyone in the ballpark knew he had blown the call. Musial never said a word, gave his bat to the ball boy, asked the ball boy to bring him his glove, and without looking at Harvey, said "Young man. I don't know what league you came here from, but home plate is 17 inches wide in this league, same as it is in every other league." Doug Harvey decided right then to never again anticipate a call. He would look at a play, make a decision, and then make the call. He controlled the game on the field, never allowed any nonsense, went strictly by the rules, and had such a commanding presence on the field that all of the players, coaches, and managers respectfully nicknamed him *God*. Tommy Lasorda, the manager of the Los Angeles Dodgers, hollered out to Harvey one time that the other team was intimidating him. Harvey called time, walked over to the Dodgers dugout, and said, "Mr. Lasorda, nobody intimidates me." When it was announced that Doug Harvey was going to be inducted onto the Baseball Hall of Fame, Tommy Lasorda called up and asked if he could speak at the ceremony. He said, "I've called umpires a lot of names, and I've called Doug a lot of names, but I always considered it a privilege to be on the same field when Doug Harvey was calling a game. If I couldn't have flown here today to speak, I would have crawled here."

Ted Turner inherited a billboard company from his father, not the most imposing start to becoming a multi-billionaire. Ted was also a total fanatic (that's where the word "fan" comes from) about the Atlanta Braves major league baseball team. Ted watched or attended every home game, but was totally frustrated in not being able to watch their games when they were on the road. Then he learned about the possibility of buying some unused bandwidth and sending a TV signal through a cable into people's homes. Despite everyone laughing at him and saying it couldn't be done, he started a cable TV company, laid cable, got subscribers to sign up, and created a new industry. Turner Network Television was born. How about a channel that only showed old movies? Turner Classic Movies was born. How about an all news channel, 24/7? CNN was born. How about a channel devoted to golf? Arnold Palmer was an early investor and the Golf Channel was born. How about a channel devoted just to weather? The Weather Channel was born. A tiny company in Windsor, CT called Electronic Sports Programming Network signed on – you may know them by their initials. A guy who worked with Ted for many years said that Ted's greatest gift was being able to imagine something new, and when Ted explained it to everyone, they would always say that that was obvious.

Jim Butcher is one of my favorite fiction writers (he is in Appendix C). He writes about a wizard in Chicago named Harry Dresden who is a warden of the White Council, gets in trouble a lot, casts spells, mixes potions, fights ghouls, has a brother who is a werewolf, travels through the underworld, has a talking skull named Bob in his laboratory and solves problems – it's not your father's fiction, so you have to open up your mind. The books have good plots and are written very well. In a recent book, Harry is teaching a class of young wizards-to-be about how to approach an investigation: when you know what you are facing, you can then figure out how to deal with it. He calls it the 4 A's, to which he adds a 5th A:

- Ascertain – what is the problem?
- Analyze – why is it happening? Read, learn, talk
- Assemble – what should you do? Plan, determine consequences of actions
- Act – it's a gamble. Realize that you don't know everything
- The 5th A that Harry adds is Arrogance – you think you've figured it out but you haven't. Pride gets in your way. You must have the honesty to reassess.

XIII

EVERYONE'S # 1 FEAR – PUBLIC SPEAKING

At some point in your career, and if you expect to have any degree of success, many times you will have to stand up in front of a group of people and talk. It is the single biggest fear that the vast majority of people, both male and female, possess and want to avoid. I was extremely fortunate – my first boss at my first job out of college told me that I should go to Toastmasters. I learned how to talk in front of a group, to prepare and give 5 minute speeches, to give impromptu talks, to tell jokes on command, and to quit saying *UH*. It was a fabulous experience.

George Bernard Shaw: "The single biggest problem in communications is the illusion that it has taken place."

To make it even worse, this form of communication is very delicate, being solely dependent on one person talking and the other person or persons listening. Any little thing can interrupt this exchange. A mosquito with sore feet, landing on a cotton ball, can make so much noise that it will destroy the concentration of the audience and make it impossible for them to hear you. The slightest noise, shadow, movement, or distraction can be devastating. This is the main justification for repeating yourself often.

We have been given 5 senses to work with when we are in an audience:

- We can't touch the words,
- We can't taste the words, and
- We can't smell the words (well, hopefully not).

So we're left with hearing and seeing. And human beings absolutely cannot do both at the same time.

I don't care if it's a flipchart, a poster, writing on a whiteboard, or the relentless overuse of a Power Point slide show, it's a war between the speaker and the audience to get them to listen to you. As a speaker, you have to do everything in your power to keep the audience's attention focused on you, the speaker.

Here are some proven techniques:

- Gestures – flail away and use your arms for emphasis – look at me !
- Nail your feet to the floor – if you wander around, their eyes will follow you and their ears won't.
- Try the U. S. Army approach: tell them what you're going to tell them, tell them, and then tell them what you told them.
- Experienced speakers repeat things often – just keep trying to break through – different skulls have different thicknesses.
- *NEVER* dim the lights. ZZZZZZZZ.

- Vary the volume, pitch, and cadence of your voice – death to the monotone.
- Speak slowly and clearly. Enunciate. Enunciate.
- Be especially sensitive if English is not the 1st language for the audience.
- Avoid needlessly multi-syllabic words. You're not there to impress them with your vocabulary but to communicate with them.
- *SLOW DOWN* ! The most obvious sign of nerves is being in such a rush to get the words out that the audience can't understand you. It's not a contest of the most words per minute.

Just before my first presentation in the New York office to the company president and his vice-presidents, my new boss stopped me out in the hallway. He said, "Just pretend that everyone in the room is sitting on the toilet with their pants down around their ankles. They're just human beings like you and me and there's nothing to be afraid of."

- Before you say your first word, tell yourself the most crude, profane, funniest joke you have ever heard. Then you can start talking with a smile on your face and a positive attitude. Your audience can read your face.
- State at the beginning by stating that no dumb questions exist. All questions are legitimate and may be asked at any time.
- Tell them that the most important thing they need to know at the start is the location of the rest rooms.
- Take a break every hour – they need to go potty and they need a break from listening to you.
- After every break, solicit questions.

- Somewhere in the Middle East, I was asked what a rest room was. They thought it was a place to take a nap. I carefully used the word "toilet" thereafter.
- If you're writing on a flipchart, turn the page when you're done.
- If you're writing on a whiteboard, erase it when you're done.
- If you give them something to look at, they will look and not listen.
- Power Point is a great tool, but don't use it as a crutch.
- Don't insult your audience by reading slides to them. They can read.
- Only flash up a slide to talk about it – minimum information.
- You want to keep the focus on you – the speaker.
- A bullet point means just that - not a phrase - not a sentence - not a paragraph.
- A single word or a single number is fine on a slide – just talk about it – minimize distractions.
- Remote controls on a projector have a button that will black out the screen – wear it out.
- Assuming the projector and laptop are tied together, pressing the letter "B" on your laptop will black out the screen.
- All of the above tips selfishly force the audience to listen to you, the speaker. Be ruthless, nicely.
- Check out the meeting room the night before.
- Be ready to start at least 30 minutes early to be sure everything works.
- Always carry a long extension cord with you.
- Are the words on the screen legible from the back of the room?

- Find the person responsible for the equipment in the room, tip them, and find out how to find them when something goes wrong. Because something will go wrong. Bulbs burn out.
- I carried a projector with me because I knew it was compatible with my laptop. The projector provided with the room may not work with your laptop.
- My projector and laptop both died in the middle of a seminar once. I don't remember the country. I do remember that the electrical receptacles had a switch on them that had to be turned on to make the receptacles work. *I DON'T KNOW WHY* ! When the laptop battery ran down, I was dead in the water.
- One time, I turned on my laptop and had a totally black screen. Not knowing what else to do, I typed in my ID and password and everything worked. After that, I carried a flash drive as backup. You can always borrow a laptop.
- *NEVER* turn your back to the audience. It's just rude.
- *NEVER* walk between the projector and the screen. It's just rude and you might trip on something.
- Do stand at the door, welcome people, and pass out business cards.
- Pick out a person on the front left, front right, back left, and back right, and take turns looking at them as you talk. It will then appear to the audience that you're speaking to each of them individually.
- *NEVER* read a speech. I can't stand Chuck Schumer looking down his nose through his glasses and reading a speech to me. The optics are terrible. Is your memory so poor that you can't remember what you're going to say?
- Talk as if you were having a conversation with a friend.

123

- When you mess up or make a mistake, don't bring attention to it. Take a drink of water. Repeat a prior point that you want to emphasize.
- Don't overshare. Personal, self-deprecating stories make you look human, but avoid TMI.
- Be patient. The rest of the world is not as anal as Americans and may not be prompt.
- Do stand at the door at the end of the presentation, and thank each person for attending.

XIV

YOU NEED TO LEARN TO WRITE

a. CARRY A DIARY - USE A DIARY

It will be a useful reference for you if you keep a diary that you write in every day. Keeping track of what you were doing and working on each day is good mental discipline. It doesn't have to be anything fancy, just a spiral notebook works just fine. Carry a small notebook in your pocket because you never know when *INSPIRATION* will strike, and you won't remember everything.

b. WRITE UP NOTES ON EVERY MEETING AND TRIP

They will also be useful references of who you saw and what you talked about, which you will use in the future.

c. JOE BOB BRIGGS ARTICLE

I read a free weekly newspaper that is printed in Dallas called *The Dallas Observer.* It's somewhat funky, off the wall, occasionally hilarious, but always interesting. John Bloom created a character named Joe Bob Briggs (notice the double first name) who reviewed "B" movies and created a job for himself as the "Drive-In Movie Critic." He originally wrote for the Dallas Times-Herald, a former daily newspaper, and was fired after a tongue-in-cheek review of *We Are the World* entitled *We Are the Weird* wasn't appreciated.

I saved his article from the 23 May 1991 edition entitled *How To Write* because it was not only funny but made a lot of sense, and I quote it here:

"About 5 years ago, people started asking me how to write, friends, mostly.

"I've got this great idea for a book. All I need to know is how to get it in shape."

Or "I'm planning to be a writer. Do you have any advice on where I could start out?"

Or sometimes I would get invitations to speak at writer's conferences or journalism conventions or university seminars on weighty topics like *The Modern Humorous Essay.* And I would go to cocktail parties where bitter white wine was served in plastic glasses by women with 2 last names. And, for a while, when I first got these invitations, I would actually accept them and go spend a day spouting off about this thing and that thing and the other thing. And people would *take notes* on the stuff

I was saying. And when aspiring writers wrote me letters, I would write them back, volunteering suggestions on how to write and when to write and so on and so forth. And the aspiring writers would write me back, so *grateful* for what I had told them.

And then, one day, I realized…

I didn't know what the heck I was talking about.

If you met me during this Blabbermouth period of my life, then you already *realize*, of course that I didn't know what the heck I was talking about. But this realization didn't hit me until much later.

Now, I'm trying to make up for it. I know practically *nothing* about the science, or art, or craft, of writing. But this column contains *everything* that I know beyond a doubt.

1. *The way you become a writer is you write. Every day. No exception.*
    Nobody believes this. Everybody wants to believe in something called *talent* or *inspiration* or the *knack for it*. Maybe there is such a thing, but it has nothing to do with becoming a writer. So when someone says "I wanna be a writer — what do I do?" the first thing I say is "Go and write for 2 hours a day for 2 weeks, and then bring me what you've written."
    To a professional writer, this is a very *light* writing schedule. But 99% of them will vanish forever.
    It's too mundane. Nobody believes it.

2. *What you write is not important.*
Nobody believes this either. Most people think "If I could just get the right *idea*, then the writing would flow. That's like saying "If Nolan Ryan would just throw me the right pitch, then I could hit home runs for the Yankees." Before you get the chance to face the big pitch from Nolan Ryan, you have to hit 200,000 other pitches. Every day. No exceptions.
The ideas don't matter. The practice matters.

3. *Nobody is going to steal your idea.*
Everybody who is about to write a book is afraid that they tell someone (like me) the topic, and 6 months later Doubleday will be bringing out a 200,000 first printing on the *same* topic, but written by Norman Mailer, and the aspiring writer's chance for celebrity will be dashed.
Listen up. You don't get widely plagiarized until you're widely published – and then it doesn't matter. Trust me on this.

4. *There are no new ideas.* There are only individual expressions of old ideas. If you and I write the same thing, it will come out in 2 versions so different that no one will notice, but *both* versions will be extremely similar to things written 3000 years ago. To put it another way, your imagination doesn't belong to you – it's just something you're entrusted with for a time.

5. *Be honest. It always works.*

6. *Don't listen to anybody's opinions about what you write, especially your friends and family.* (I don't mean ignore these people. I mean listen to the voice inside you that

says *That's good* and *That stinks.* It's the only voice that doesn't lie.)

7. *Never be afraid to write something that stinks.* The more stinky stuff you put out, the more risks you take. And the more risks you take, the better chance you have of creating something beautiful. No great writer has ever been a wimp.

8. *If you can explain how to write a book, then you don't know how to write one.* If you can write a book, then you won't be able to explain how you did it. It's stupid, but it's true.

   There are no rules about what to write, how to write it, or what will *sell.* Never ask a book publisher what will *sell.* They're the last to know.

9. *There are no membership cards or initiation rites for this profession.* Anybody with a sheet of paper can do it. So you become a writer on the day you say *I'm a writer.* It doesn't matter where your income comes from. The work you take joy from is writing.

10. *Nobody can tell you how to write, but there are certain things you can do to get to a place where you can write.* There are 3 of them:

    Write every day.

    Write every day.

    Write every day.

    This is all I know.

XV

BUSINESS TRAVEL

a. TRAVEL IN THE U.S.A.

I've been in 49 states and there's a reason why they call Iowa the *fly-over* state. Sorry, Iowa. I'll get there someday. Here are some simple guidelines that will make your life less stressful.

Trips by Automobile:

- Set the cruise control on the speed limit and get in the right hand lane. You won't save that much time by driving faster. There's nothing a state trooper likes more than stopping someone for speeding and they have an out-of-state driver's license. You don't want to be introduced to the local justice-of-the-peace who will ask you if you think you're in Indianapolis. And no, he doesn't take American Express. Ka-ching !
- Listen to calm music. Soothe your soul. You won't drive as fast.
- Turn your phones off. Very few true emergencies occur and you can't do anything about them when you're

driving anyway. You can always check your messages when you stop somewhere for one of your frequent rest stops.

- Wear dark clothes. Spilled food and drinks will not show up as vividly. It will happen.
- Pack an extra change of clothes (see above) as your plans could change.
- Have a paper copy of a map and directions to where you are going. A GPS can die or be wrong. It's embarrassing to have to call up your customer or client and ask how to get to their office. It smells of incompetence – why should they use you or your company if you can't even get to their offices?
- Traveler's checks are a worthless nuisance.
- Take $500 in cash on each trip and keep it in your clothes, your socks, your shoes, and your briefcase. Cash is king. Hoard it for when you truly need it.
- Carry at least 2 credit cards from which you can get cash at an ATM, when needed. You will at some point need a backup. Computer systems can go down, banks can have screwups, power outages occur, and only when you are traveling.
- Always use credit cards for all of your purchases whenever possible, for 2 reasons: it creates a paper trail that you may need to reference when creating your expense account and it conserves cash.
- Get receipts whenever possible for all purchases. There was a traveling salesman who asked his waitress to put tomorrow's date on the receipt for dinner because he had already used up today yesterday.
- Make a habit, every evening, of listing all of your expenses for that day. Excel spreadsheets work well,

and even old-fashioned pencil-and-paper still works. It would be terminally stupid to lose money on a trip because you forgot to write something down.

- Don't schedule appointments too close together. You don't want to shut down visits because you need to be somewhere else. Bad optics and a worse impression. You never know what a client or customer will tell you or what they need. There is no opportunity greater than sitting across the desk from someone and listening.

Trips by Airplane:

Your first question to ask yourself is do I fly or do I drive? It's a major hassle and time killer to fly in the U.S. My breakeven point was 4 hours – if I could drive there in 4 hours, that was about how long it would take from my house to my destination if I flew. More than 4 hours, I would head to the airport. Additional guidelines for flying in the U.S.:

- Don't wear shoes with laces. Security lines are long enough without having to fool with laces.
- I always check a bag. Planes are getting very limited on space inside the cabin. I usually had a laptop, a CPAP machine, and luggage, so I didn't want to drag all that stuff onto and off of an airplane.

b. TRAVEL OUTSIDE U.S.A.

- You won't realize that the U.S. is the best country in the world until you get out of it.
- Only differences are the length of the flight and everyone talks funny.

- Jetways are not common outside of US and western Europe. Be prepared to climb up and down ramps and flights of stairs.
- When in a foreign country, remember that you're the foreigner, not all of them.
- Always assume that everyone understands and is able to speak some English, so be careful what you say.
- Take $1,000 in cash with you on each trip. I once had a hotel in Africa and a hotel in rural Russia, in succession, that didn't accept credit cards, I ended up in Moscow on a Sunday morning with no cash, and the story got worse from there on. You can figure out how to survive.
- You handle jet lag by never laying down and taking a short nap. Stay on your feet, walk, drink caffeine, and stay up until supper time. Eat supper and then stay awake as long as you can. You should be fine the next day.
- Don't ever try to do any business the day you arrive. You'll hit a wall in the afternoon and not be able to think.
- Drink lots of water. You'll be dehydrated from the plane ride.
- Get rid of your U. S. bias. It's inbred and unconscious but it's still there.
- Try to fit into their culture as quickly as you can. Regardless of how clearly and how loudly you speak English to someone, they still may not understand you at all. It's not their fault !
- Learn the local word for toilet as soon as possible. Everything else is less important.

- Go sightseeing. You may never get the chance to be back in that city.
- Write thank-you notes to your hosts after each visit.
- Write up trip notes to yourself after each visit – they will be a valuable resource later.
- Have 2 passports – it's perfectly legal; very handy if going in and out of Israel; also very handy if you need to mail off one passport to get a visa while you are using the other passport to travel somewhere.
- Carry paper copies of everything.

XVI

WHAT TO DO WHEN YOU LOSE YOUR JOB?

It would be nice to think that you could go to work for a company, have increasingly important and rewarding job responsibilities, and eventually retire from that company into a comfortable old age. If you believe that, you are living in a fantasy, because the real world is very different.

At the start of the movie *Patton*, George C. Scott reprised most of Patton's famous speech to his troops. If you read the speech, one portion that was omitted from the movie was when Patton told his troops that 2% of them were going to die in the war. "Those are just the grim, gruesome, and horrible realities, for both sides, in a war. My job is to minimize that number as much as I can, while still defeating the enemy."

I would estimate that in the rapid technological advancement and obsolescence of the current workforce, maybe 2% of you might work for the same employer until you retire. The prudent person (and aren't we all prudent) would prepare for change in the following ways:

1. Develop and actively nurture your network of former classmates, professional organizations, former teachers, former co-workers, former bosses, relatives, friends, tennis partners, bridge partners, poker partners, golf partners, etc. and stay in touch with all of them. Trust me, you never know where your next job will come from.

2. When, not if, you lose your job, you immediately have a new job – finding your next job ! Nothing else is more important. Get after it ! You're burning daylight !

3. Assume that every lost job is a blessing. You don't know it yet but you're going to meet and work with new people, have new experiences, maybe work in new industries. You would have missed so much by staying in the comfortable little pigeon-hole that you were in.

4. Planning out your life is pretty useless because the world doesn't co-operate with the way you have it planned out. God laughs. Be prepared for and welcome change because it's really good news disguised as a disruption in your life. The Aussies have a saying, "Don't get your knickers in a knot !"

5. Forget looking at newspaper ads – it's a waste of your time.

6. Forget search firms or agencies – they're searching for your wallet.

7. Don't ask friends or acquaintances for a job – you just put them in a very awkward spot.

8. Do tell friends and acquaintances that you're looking for a job and ask them to let you know about situations that might fit your skills and background.

9. I've had 9 different jobs in 36 years in Dallas, all through people I knew.

10. Never turn down an interview – look at it as practice and a chance to learn.

11. Lock your pride in a closet. Don't mope. Don't delay.

12. Reverse the process and interview the companies to see if you want to work with them.

13. Work diligently to keep your sense of humor alive and well.

14. *NEVER BURN ANY BRIDGES* !

15. Your new job is finding a job – it's hard work – focus on doing it every day.

16. Don't hide at home. You can read books and take naps later.

17. Mix at parties, job fairs, and bars – fate can step in.

18. Recruit your friends and family to help you search – they will gladly do it.

19. *NETWORK, NETWORK, NETWORK* !

20. Mail out paper resumes through snail mail. The recipient will have to physically do something with the envelope and the resume.

21. Electronic messages with an attached resume are too easy to delete.

22. Don't use white paper – it looks cheap. You want your resume to stand out in a crowd.

23. A chronological tour of your life may not be the best approach to attracting a job offer.

24. Describe how your experience can help their company – what character traits should make you attractive to them.

25. Describe the job you want and explain how it could help your prospective employer.

26. Your desired job may not yet exist, until you explain it to them, but new jobs are created every day.

27. Sell yourself as a problem solver – every company needs them – give examples – solutions to problems are not industry specific.
28. Make yourself a list, maybe to share, of strengths (assets) and weaknesses (liabilities).
29. Start planning your next job while you still have your current job. What do you need to know? Who do you need to know?

XVII

COLLECTION OF ANECDOTES THAT ALL HAVE A POINT, LESSON, MESSAGE, AND/OR MORAL

Clint Eastwood - Every movie that Clint has made with Warner Brothers has been on a handshake agreement, never a contract. They've gotten mad at each other and walked away, but always get back together and figure out how to make it work. Clint has never had a contract with a lawyer nor an agent, just handshake agreements. And he's worked with the same people for over 40 years. "If you don't trust each other, what good is a piece of paper? We're not going to court, we'll figure it out." Oh, and Clint writes all the music for his movies.

After all the years I've spent in the corporate world, I've become disillusioned with the importance of contracts. You want to do business with another company for one reason — so that both of you can make a profit. If the situation becomes untenable for either side, you will sit down and talk about it. You need each other to make the transaction work. Suing each other and spending a lot of time in court and money on lawyers is very unproductive and drawn out and a waste for both sides.

Let's take an example of a brewery adjacent to a company that makes aluminum cans. They will work out their problems because one can't sell beer without the other one making cans. They have mutual interests. They need each other. They're not going to court and fight and kick either one out because that would put a serious dent in their sales, no pun intended. If both of them live up to their word, there is no need for a contract. It's really an intent to do business with each other, not to each other. The only time you need a contract is to figure out damages when either side breaks their word.

Churchill in Prison – It happened during the Boer War in what is now South Africa, as described by Candice Millard in *Hero of the Empire* (Doubleday, 2016) in what reads like a James Bond novel. An escape from prison and 300 miles from the nearest British consulate in Portuguese East Africa, walking by night, hiding by day, hidden in a coal mine by the English mine manager, hidden in a rail car of wool, and finally walking up to the consulate at 3AM and told to come back in the morning. A fascinating book.

Read about Winston Churchill's life – it's a very inspiring story about perseverance

- Abandoned in Blenheim Castle as a child
- Raised by a nanny (he kept a picture of her in his bedroom his entire life)
- A poor and disinterested student
- Got into Britain's military academy on his 3rd try
- POW in South Africa

- Served as a soldier all over the world
- Fought in trenches in World War I
- Invented the tank
- Totally froze and panicked when trying to make his 1ˢᵗ speech in Parliament
- Lone voice in England warning about danger of Nazi Germany
- Had childhood dream of becoming Prime Minister of England
- Saved England and perhaps Western civilization by force of will

A fascinating person, described in 3 volumes by William Manchester.

The first 2 words in every e-mail or letter that you send to everyone should be "Thank you" – flatter them a little, get on their good side, be grateful for their communication or their business with you.

Herb Kelleher & Southwest Airlines - Herb was the company lawyer when he and some buddies started out with 2 airplanes. His wife refused to move from San Antonio to Dallas so Herb commuted to work every day. Gate 1 at Love Field in Dallas was reserved for flights to San Antonio and Herb did his market research by talking to passengers, never hired any focus groups or conducted surveys, just trusted his gut.

I used to eat lunch at a greasy spoon at the end of the runway at Love Field called *Club Schmitz*: gravel parking lot, pool tables, shuffleboard, great food if you liked it fried. I went back just before it finally closed after over 60 years and noticed a plaque on the wall thanking Herb for his patronage – he ate lunch there every day with the mechanics for the airline.

I was fortunate to see Herb in action once in Tulsa, an 8AM flight to Dallas in July that was delayed several times by mechanical problems, and finally cancelled. They flew another plane in from Dallas and by then we were a sweaty band of travelers ready to explode. After we got on the replacement plane, the stewardess told us that there would be another short delay as Herb Kelleher, the president of the airline would be on the plane, and there would be a *social delay*. Translated, Herb was having a cigarette in the maintenance shop. I happened to be sitting near the front of the plane and saw Herb coming down the jetway, snapping his fingers, whistling, not a care in the world. The stewardess met him at the door and said, "Herb, we've got a plane-load of very unhappy passengers." "Don't worry, I'll take care of that" and he took the tray of peanuts from her, went to every passenger on the plane with a big smile on his face, shook their hands, thanked them for flying on Southwest Airlines, made 150 new friends, and completely turned around the attitude of everyone on the plane in 10 minutes. He saw a problem, knew he could do something about it, and did it. One of the most amazing things I've ever seen. I was blown away.

The Oddity of President Trump - Forget politics and personalities and think about what just happened:

- 15 Republican candidates on a stage and Donald Trump says, "I think I'll run for President", so they have to scrounge up another microphone.
- No campaign staff, no political background, playboy of the Western world.

- Didn't act or talk like any other candidate before.
- All the political pundits and so-called "experts" just laughed.
- He wins the first primary.
- He appealed to something in enough voters to keep winning primaries.
- He gets the nomination.
- "Oh, there's no way. Hillary has this election sewed up. He doesn't have a chance."
- He wins the election.
- Have you thought about what we just saw?
- Ignore the person, think about the accomplishment. Is there a lesson for you in your life? Have you ever been faced with seemingly insurmountable odds? What did you do about it?
- Ain't America great?

A research scientist was working on a new formula for insecticides when he accidentally licked his finger and it tasted sweet. Why a guy working on insecticides would lick his finger is beyond me, but he had just discovered the artificial sweetener called aspartame which is marketed as Sweet-N-Lo and is contained in many foods and beverages.

A guy at 3M was working on a new type of glue which was a failure. Pieces of paper would stick together but easily pull apart – not a permanent bonding. He decided to cut his failed project into small rectangles and used them to mark his hymnal for the choir he sang in every Sunday. Soon, the other members of the choir wanted pieces of the failed sticky paper for their hymnals. I was in Boise, ID in the early 1980's when 3M first test marketed Post-It-Notes.

Lawrence Rawl worked in the supply department of Humble Oil & Refining Company in the early 1970's, a precursor to Exxon. One day, he went up to the room where the Board of Directors were meeting and asked for his boss. His boss was quite perturbed to be pulled out of the meeting. Rawl said, "I have a contract that needs to be approved." His boss said, "Larry, I can't do that. It needs to be discussed and analyzed and put on the agenda." Rawl said, "OK, but it's costing us $100,000 a day until I get it approved." The point is that he wasn't shy about interrupting a board meeting if he thought it was important. When he became board chairman, some procedures got changed.

A researcher at Corning Glass works was working with a new formula for glass. He put a sample in an oven, thought he had set it for 600F, went to lunch, and discovered when he got back that the oven was at 900F and his sample was red hot. He quickly grabbed some tongs, tried to get the sample out of the oven, dropped it on the concrete floor, and it didn't break. When the sample cooled off, it had turned white. He had just invented CorningWare. He later was fooling with samples of a glass that turned gray when exposed to bright light – he had just invented Varilux lenses.

James Joyce, the great Irish poet, was found by a friend one day slumped over his writing desk. "James, are you all right?" No answer. "James, is it the writing?" "Yes." "Well, what have you written today?" "Only 7 words." "Well, 7 words is good for you." "Yes, it is, but I don't know what order they should go in."

Two guys go on a sales call and it does not go well, a borderline disaster. In the elevator leaving the building, one guy says,

"Why is it that people take such an instant dislike to me?" The other guy says, "It's simple. It saves time."

Thomas Edison said he wasn't a great inventor – he had just tested 10,000 things that didn't work.

James Watson, co-discoverer of DNA: "It's necessary to be slightly under-employed to accomplish something." I took this to mean that if all you're doing is busywork, all you'll get done is busywork.

Thomas Edison again: "Hell, there are no rules here, we're trying to get something done."

Sparky Anderson was a long-time manager in major league baseball and was the 1st manager to win a World Series with teams from both leagues:

- A baseball manager is a necessary evil.
- Success is the person who year after year reaches the highest limits in their field.
- People who live in the past are generally afraid to compete in the present.
- Just give me 25 guys on the last year of their contract and I'll win you a pennant every year.
- Me carrying a briefcase is like a hotdog wearing earrings.
- A manager never won a pennant.
- If I ever find a pitcher with a great fastball, a good curveball, and a slider, I might consider marrying him, or at least proposing.
- I wouldn't embarrass any catcher by comparing them to Johnny Bench.

- Sparky holds the record for the shortest visit to the mound to talk to a struggling pitcher: "Babe Ruth's dead. Throw strikes."
- The secret to being a successful big league manager is to keep the 5 guys that hate you away from the 5 guys who are undecided.

Leonard Lauder (Estee's son): "Never ask for permission. Beg for forgiveness."

Vince Lombardi: "Sometimes you work so hard at something you can't accept any outcome other than winning."

Steve Jobs: "Deciding what not to do is as important as deciding what to do."

Paul McCartney once had writer's block for over 2 years, not a word, not a note. He had a dream one night, woke up, and wrote down the words and music to *Yesterday* in a single draft, never changed a word or a note. It's the single most-recorded song in history. Sorry, folks. Talent like that can't be taught.

Sir Elton John and his collaborator, Bernie Taupin, communicate by fax machine. Elton lives in London and Bernie lives in Los Angeles. Bernie writes the words and Elton writes the music. Don't knock it. It's worked for 50 years.

Did you ever feel like a country dog in the city? If you stand still, they'll screw you. If you run, they'll bite you in the butt.

Vince Lombardi again: "The harder you work, the harder it is to quit."

Mike Trout, sensational center fielder for Los Angeles Angels: "I always take the 1st pitch so that I can see the ball coming out of the pitcher's hand." One of his coaches says Trout is the best he has ever seen at how quickly he can recognize a pitch as soon as it leaves the pitcher's hand. "The best part of hitting? You have control of what you're doing. You're in the batter's box. It's your box. I love hitting. You put in all the time and practice to go out there and put up good numbers, and it's just so fun. I enjoy it so much. Guys on base get me excited." "Hold on", he's told. "The pitcher is the one in control. He's got the baseball. He's the one who knows where it's going, how fast it's going, how it's spinning – you can only react to what the pitcher does." Trout says, "I flip it. I know my zone. It's my batter's box. If you give the pitcher anything, it just gives him an advantage and an edge. So you have to go in that box and own it. Think positive and it's yours." In his first 6 seasons in the major leagues, he has been the MVP 2 times, finished 2nd 3 times, and finished 4th once. The 2018 season is his best ever, both offensively and defensively.

Bobbi Brown: "Be who you are. Everyone else is already taken."

Read the book *"How We Got To Now"* (see Appendix D). It may be painful reading because you will have to do some thinking about 6 topics: Glass, Cold, Sound, Clean, Time, and Light. But you will enjoy this fascinating journey.

Walter Mosley: "Whoever you are, you have to love what you do, or you end up hating yourself."

Sign on the back of a dump truck in Lampasas, TX: "There's nothing like a good dump." Wisdom appears in the strangest of places. Stay alert. Keep looking.

Dwayne Johnson (The Rock): "When your back is against the wall, the only direction to go is forward."

Johnny Bench was the catcher for the Cincinnati Reds and Gerry Arrigo was pitching. Bench signaled for a curveball – Arrigo wanted to throw a fastball. Bench again signaled for a curveball – Arrigo again wanted to throw a fastball. Eventually Arrigo threw a fastball and Bench caught it barehanded and flipped it back to him. Message sent. Message received.

Jerry Brown, Governor of California, on his "canoe theory of politics": "You paddle a little bit to the left, then you paddle a little bit to the right, and you end up paddling a straight course, with help from both sides."

The 3 stages of life: Youth, middle age, and "You're looking good !"

Gary McCord is an announcer for CBS at many golf tournaments. When he was playing on the Senior tour, he woke up one morning at 2AM and thought he was having a heart attack. The only guy he knew (who shall remain nameless) that was staying at his hotel was a fellow golfer and a legendary drinker. Gary called him and told him that he needed a ride to a hospital. This guy told Gary he would pick him up in front of the hotel, and drove the biggest Cadillac that was made. Gary crawled into the back seat, which felt as big as a living room couch. As they were driving to the hospital, his friend (who hiccupped when he drank) told Gary he had figured out what was wrong with his golf game. Gary was in tremendous pain and not that interested, but kindly said, "What's wrong with your golf game?" "Well, (hic) I've finally (hic) figured out that (hic) I've been practicing (hic) sober and playing (hic) drunk !"

Steve Jobs: "My model for business is the Beatles. They were 4 guys who kept each other's negative tendencies in check. They balanced each other and the total was greater than the sum of the parts. That's how I see business. Great things are never done by one person. They're done by a team of people."

Allen Murray was born and raised in Brooklyn. Education was not stressed in his home so he dropped out of high school and joined the Army. Given some standard tests, he found out his IQ was off the charts. "I never knew I was smart." After the Army, he got a job in the mail room at Mobil Oil Company and finished high school. After 10 years of night school, he earned a degree in accounting. He retired as chairman of the board of Mobil Corporation. Very few career paths are straight lines.

Steve Jobs again: "People don't know what they want until you show it to them."

Unknown: "Socialism works great until you've given away everyone's money. Then you become Venezuela."

Bill Gates on Steve Jobs: "Don't you understand that Steve doesn't know anything about technology. He is a super salesman. He doesn't know anything about engineering and 99% of what he says and thinks is wrong."

Vince Gill was a guitar player in Emmy Lou Harris' band. After a few years, he came to her and said he wanted to go out on his own. She told him she had been wondering when he was going to do that because he had been ready for some time. "Why didn't you say something?" "I couldn't. You had to make that decision for yourself. You had to own it. You had to live it. No one can do that for you."

James Watson again: "One could not be a successful scientist without realizing that, in contrast to the popular perception supported by the media and the mothers of scientists, a large number of scientists are not only narrow-minded and dull, but also stupid and unmotivated."

Willie Nelson was asked if he could live his life over again, would he change anything? "No. I'm sorry that I hurt some people and disappointed others. But if I had not had all those experiences, both good and bad, and met all of the people I've met, I wouldn't be the person I am today and would not have been able to write all the songs I've written. So no, I wouldn't change a thing."

Kristoffer Kristofferson was an army brat, raised on army bases all over the world. His father, Lars, was in the Army Air Corps and eventually became a major general in the U.S. Air Force. Kris graduated from Pomona College in California and went to Oxford as a Rhodes Scholar. He dutifully joined the family business by enlisting in the Army, went to Ranger school, learned to fly helicopters, and with Vietnam in the rear view mirror was assigned as a captain to teach English Literature at West Point. At age 37, he resigned and drove to Nashville to become a songwriter. No one in his family ever spoke to him again. He lived in his car for a while, met Johnny Cash and Willie Nelson in a recording studio where he was trying to sell some songs he had written. Johnny let him live in a spare bedroom in his house, and the rest, as they say, is history. *Sunday Morning Coming Down, For the Good Times, Me and Bobby McGee, Help Me Make It Through the Night* and many others.

Kris has said that he spent the first 37 years of his life doing what everyone else wanted him to do and he's spent the rest of his life doing what he wanted to do. Songwriter, actor, singer, poet, author. "It's been a long strange ride."

Thomas Edison again: "I can always hire engineers and mathematicians. But they can't hire me." Genius can't be sold, only rented.

Napoleon: "When your enemy is doing something stupid, don't interfere."

Napoleon again: "I like lucky generals. The others don't seem to last long."

Pfizer, the pharmaceutical company, had contracted out some R&D work to a company in the UK on a new angina drug for elderly patients. It wasn't working very well, but the UK company noted that all the male patients were getting erections. It is an urban myth that the patients were given a pill and a warm glass of milk at night so they wouldn't roll over and fall out of bed in their sleep. They had just discovered Viagra.

Josef Stalin: "The winners write history."

Josef Stalin is found alive in a small cabin in Siberia. His many former supporters try to convince him to come back to Moscow and return Russia to its former place of prominence in the world. Stalin finally relents: "OK, but no Mr. Nice Guy this time."

Josef Stalin appears to Vladimir Putin in a dream and says, "Vladimir, do you want to stay in power?" Vladimir says, "Of course, what do I need to do?" Stalin says, "You must kill all your enemies, hang their children, assassinate all of their relatives, and paint your office blue." Vladimir says, "Why paint the office blue?"

A golfer in a senior PGA tournament was getting ready to hit his tee shot when the TV announcer said," The wind is coming out of his rear." The co-host tried to cover for him by quickly adding, "You mean the wind is blowing at his back." The other announcer ran with it, "Maybe someone is close enough to smell it." Hey, they were just commenting.

Ted Williams was arguably the best hitter ever in baseball, a lifetime batting average of .344, he hit .388 at the age of 39, and was the last person to exceed a .400 average for a season. In 1941, Ted was batting .3995 with just a doubleheader left in the season. That average would have been rounded up to .400, but Ted wasn't a round–it–up kind of guy. He went 6 for 8 in the last 2 games and finished at .406. He famously said that when the bases were loaded and the count was 3 balls and 2 strikes, he had the pitcher exactly where he wanted him. Most people would have seen that as a negative, pressure filled situation. Ted saw it as all positive: he knew the pitcher had to throw a strike, the pitcher knew he had to throw a strike, everyone in the whole ball park knew the pitcher had to throw a strike, and Ted knew that when the pitcher did throw a strike, he could hit it and hit it hard. He couldn't wait.

When Stanley McChrystal was commanding the Allied forces in 2010 in Afghanistan, he attended a news conference where reporters asked lots of questions about the war, and he gave simple, straight-forward answers that reflected his opinions. At the time, McChrystal was a 4 star Army general, the son of a major general, and had been in and around the military his entire life. When the media accounts of the news conference reached Washington, they caused great distress in the Obama White House, the President's cabinet, and Congress. President Obama ordered General McChrystal to be in his office as soon as possible. The general flew all night and appeared bright and early the next morning at the White House:

"I'm surprised you got here so quickly."

"Just following orders, Mr. President."

"Your remarks at your news conference were very upsetting here in Washington."

"I'm just a simple soldier, Mr. President. People asked me questions and I answered them."

"You're anything but a simple soldier, General, but because of your remarks at the news conference, I'm going to have to request your resignation."

McChrystal pulled said letter out of his pocket, signed, dated, and witnessed, and handed it to the President.

"So you were expecting this?"

"The President doesn't ask a 4 star to be in his office ASAP from Afghanistan unless something major was going to happen to him. My only possible promotion was to be Army Chief of Staff, that job is already taken, and you could have called me to tell me that news."

"Well, I'm not going to demote you, and I will personally make sure that you get all of the benefits and pension you have earned."

"That's very kind of you, Mr. President."

"Thank you for your service, General."

"It's been my honor and privilege, Mr. President."

"I'm sorry you'll have to go back to say your goodbyes and pack up your office."

"I've already said my goodbyes and my office is being packed as we speak."

"I bet you'd like to piss on my grave, General."

"No, Mr. President. I've been in the Army my whole life and I hate standing in lines."

President Obama cracked up and has re-told this story on several occasions.

I always wondered if this wasn't McChrystal's exit strategy all along.

Printing on a T-shirt I saw at the gym: "Jewish Film Festival of Dallas – just like Sundance, only Jewsier !"

T-shirt worn by a lady at a poker tournament: "Look pretty, play dirty !" Watch out for her.

Have you ever met an alpha female? Scary !

Jimmy Connors, world champion tennis player, on his motivation to excel: "I hate losing more than I like winning."

Nolan Ryan, a long-time major league pitcher, had a great fastball. Upon hearing a strike called, a batter turned to the home plate umpire and said, "That pitch sounded high."

MY NEW LEXUS

I just got my new Lexus RX400H and returned to the dealer the next day complaining that I couldn't figure out how the radio worked.

The salesman explained that the radio was voice activated. "Watch this", he said. "Nelson" The radio said, "Ricky or Willie?"

He said "Willie" and the radio played "On the Road Again."

I drove away happy, and for the next several days, every time I said "Beethoven" I'd get beautiful classical music, and if I said "Beatles", I'd get one of their awesome songs.

One day, a couple ran a red light and nearly ruined my beautiful new car, but I swerved in time to avoid them. I yelled *"ASSHOLES* !"

The French national anthem began to play, sung by Jane Fonda and Michael Moore, backed up by John Kerry on guitar, Al Gore on drums, Bill Clinton on sax, and Ted Kennedy on booze.

Damn, I LOVE this car !

The greatest lead sentence ever written for a sports story was by Gary Cartwright, a writer for several Texas newspapers and Texas Monthly magazine. "Outlined against a cold, gray November sky, the Four Horsemen of the Apocalypse ride again: Famine, War, Pestilence, and Meredith."

Abraham Lincoln, upon being told that General U.S. Grant had been observed drinking whiskey replied, "Find out what he's drinking and send a bottle to each of my other generals."

Christopher Columbus was a very lucky man:

- When he left, he didn't know where he was going
- When he got there, he didn't know where he was
- When he got back, he didn't know where he had been
- And he did it all with borrowed money.

My boss and I had taken some customers to a very nice restaurant and received extremely poor service: inattentive, long waits, cold food, etc. At the end of the meal, he asked for the manager and told him, "I want to leave a tip. Do you have change for a dime?"

Willie Nelson was a session guitar player and struggling songwriter in Nashville. He met Patsy Cline's husband in a bar and played him a song he had just written. Patsy's husband insisted that Willie go with him to their house, woke up Patsy, and had Willie play the song for her. He did, she loved it, and *Crazy* became one of her biggest hits.

I had just moved to the New York office and while on a business trip back in Texas, had received a speeding ticket. When I got back to the office, young, dumb, and naïve, I approached my boss and asked him where to put a speeding ticket on my expense account. He looked over the top of his glasses and said, "Anybody that's too damned dumb to figure that out is too damned dumb to work for me." Yes, sir. Message received. He never believed in making money on a business trip, but he also never saw any reason to lose money on a business trip.

One of the big influences in my life as a kid growing up in the 1950's were the Hardy Boys mystery books, which were to young boys what Nancy Drew mystery books were to girls. The father of the Hardy Boys, Fenton Hardy, was a police detective and always stressed to his sons the importance of seeing details, small things that can have great meaning. It seemed so cool to me to practice that, and it still does.

Jay Pharoah: "I'm like a piñata – just busting open with all of this talent."

More people move to Texas than to any other state.

Jordan Spieth on his first impression of being a professional golfer on the PGA tour: "I wasn't surprised by all of the long putts that were made, because I had seen that on TV. I was very surprised by how close all the misses were."

Gordie Howe was a long-time professional hockey player for the Detroit Red Wings. He was 6'3" tall and over 200 pounds when all the other hockey players were much smaller. Gordie always skated within a 10 foot diameter circle on the ice for the simple reason that if any opponent got inside that circle, Gordie would beat the crap out of him. When a hockey player scores 3 goals in one game, it is known as a *hat trick* because the fans, who mostly wore hats back then, would excitedly throw their hats on the ice in celebration and to honor the player. A Gordie Howe hat trick was known as a goal, an assist, and a fight in the same game.

If a lawyer manages to simultaneously do something that is immoral, unethical, and illegal, it's known as a *legal hat trick*. Sorry, lawyers, I just had to throw that one in. Well, not that sorry.

I had a Catholic roommate in college, a nice Italian lad from Pittsburgh. He went to Confession every Friday night and went to Mass every weekend. I knew nothing about Catholicism, except for the fear, ignorance, paranoia, and fables drilled into my head from my rural Protestant background. I razzed him one Friday night as he headed to Confession by saying, "You Catholics have it made. Do anything you want all week, go to Confession, and then you're free to do anything you want until the next Friday." He said, "You don't understand, you have to try." I was so embarrassed and apologetic and have never forgotten that very brief lesson in humility and humanity.

Butch Harmon is a famous golf teacher and has mentored several prominent players on the PGA tour. He is the son of Claude Harmon, a former tour player who won the Masters tournament at Augusta, and was also a prominent golf teacher. When he was younger, Butch practiced every day, played every day, took lessons, and just never seemed to get any better. Frustrated, he went to his dad and asked him what else he could do to get better. His dad looked him in the eye and said, "Son, you're just not that good."

I was making one of my frequent trips from London to Dallas and happened to be in the 1st class section of the plane, and was the only person in 1ˢᵗ class. When I tire of reading, I listen to music. To really listen to music, I put on headphones, put on a sleep mask (so that I'm not distracted), and have a bottle of champagne or something red handy to provide inspiration and prevent dehydration. I was singing along to old rock songs and country and western songs when I felt a tap on the shoulder. It was the music police. I lifted up my sleep mask, took off my earphones, and the stewardess said, "I'm going to have to ask you to stop singing, because you're disturbing the pilot." "He can hear me in the cockpit?" "No, he's in the row behind you trying to take a nap."

There are many statues at the US Military Academy at West Point: one is of Douglas MacArthur, 5 star general, won the Medal of Honor, and he was 1ˢᵗ in his class at West Point. His father was a 5 star general, won the Medal of Honor, and was 1ˢᵗ in his class at West Point. Another statue is George Patton. It took him 5 years to get through West Point. I always thought it was a humorous comparison – an over-achiever and a guy who struggled. I later learned why it took Patton 5 years to get through West Point: he flunked his freshman year because he was dyslexic (maybe before the word was even invented). He had a roommate who read the material to him and he memorized everything.

Dwight Eisenhower walked into a staff meeting during World War II and the room was in an uproar. Fearing some catastrophe, he asked what was going on? "Patton has raced far ahead of the other supporting troops, has out-run his supply lines, and is not following the plans we put together!" Ike said, "Sounds like we need to get George some more gasoline." He was not minimizing all the staff work that had been done and did not criticize Patton. He was simply reminding them that they were there to win a war, not to follow a plan.

Byron Nelson on what it takes to succeed on the PGA tour: "Survive the par 3s, occasionally birdie a par 4, you absolutely must birdie every par 5, and don't do anything stupid, or you won't last very long out here."

Joe Jamail's parents were Lebanese and owned a small grocery store in downtown Houston where he swept floors and stocked shelves, before and after school, and all weekend. He was 16 when he graduated from high school, decided to go to Texas A&M, and flunked his 1st semester. He then lied about his age (it was 1942 and there was a war going on), enlisted in the Marines, and fought in every major battle all the way across the Pacific. When the war was over, he decided to go to law school at the University of Texas. "I never enrolled, no one ever asked any questions, and I just started attending classes." After one year, he was bored, decided to take the bar exam, passed, and never went back to school. He opened a one-person law office and famously would never take on a client unless they first discussed the problem over a glass of whiskey. He was the lead and winning attorney for Pennzoil in their $10 billion lawsuit against Shell Oil for breach of contract in the purchase of Getty Oil. He later donated multi-millions of dollars to the University of Texas where the football team plays on Joe Jamail Field.

Charles Howell III on the difference between stroke play and match play on the PGA tour: "In match play, every shot is like it's Friday afternoon of a stroke play event, and you're trying to make the cut so you can play on the weekend and make some money."

When Sir Winston Churchill was Prime Minister, he was blatantly insulted on the floor of Parliament by a member of the opposition party. The insult was so bad that the leaders of the opposition party told the member that he had to go to the Prime Minister's house that same day and personally apologize to Sir Winston. So the chastised member drove out to Chartwell and asked to speak to Sir Winston. The butler asked him to wait while he checked. The butler came back and said, "The Prime Minister has asked that you please wait in the library for him as he is currently moving his bowels and can only handle one ★★★★ at a time."

James Mattis, the current Secretary of Defense, was head of the Marine Corps and was fired by President Obama in 2013 for some impolitic remarks. A friend of his observed, "The tougher it gets, the calmer he gets. That's a pretty rare combination."

Mattis to his troops when he first got to Iraq: "Be polite. Be courteous. But have a plan to kill everyone you meet."

Later, by Mattis, to the Iraqis: "I come in peace. I didn't bring any artillery. But I'm pleading with you, with tears in my eyes, if you ★★★★ with me, I will kill every one of you."

Mattis to Congress: "If you don't fully fund the State Department, I need to immediately buy more ammunition."

A bridge player who had just totally mis-played a hand, turned to Charles Goren, who was standing by the table, and asked him, "How would you have played that hand, Mr. Goren?" "Under an assumed name."

Someone asked Dorothy Hayden, who was Charles Goren's partner when he won many tournaments and master point championships, what it was like to play with the world's best bridge player? "Well, I don't know. Why don't you ask him?"

Larry Bird, one of the greatest basketball players in NBA history, was participating in the 3 point shooting contest at the All Star Game. He came into the locker room before the contest and shouted, " Which one of you guys is going to come in 2nd?" He won.

William Shakespeare was a falconer – he loved to train and hunt with falcons. Many falconry terms were used in his writings, are still in use today, and most people don't know their origins:

- "fed up" – a falcon has eaten so much of its prey that it just wants to find a tree, do nothing, or take a nap.
- "under my thumb" or "wrapped around a little finger" – if you tightly hold the leather thongs (jesses) tied to their feet, they can't fly.
- "haggard" – a falcon that's difficult to train or fly.
- "hood-winked" – putting a hood over a falcon's head so that it can't see.
- From "The Taming of the Shrew":
  o My falcon now is sharp and passing empty
  o And till she stoop she must not be full-gorged
  o For then she never looks upon her lure.
  o Another way I have to man my haggard,
  o To make her come and know her keeper's call.
  Reference: "The Disappearance", C. J. Box, page 219, Putnam, 2018

I was in the gate area waiting to board a flight in the Middle East when I noticed a man in the traditional white robes with a hooded falcon sitting on his leather-gloved left hand with another hooded falcon, encased in leather, laying on a table in front of him. We all got on the plane and the first falcon sat quietly on the man's wrist the entire flight. I guess he placed the other falcon under the seat in front of him.

Brad Meltzer in *The Escape Artist*: "There are many kinds of death, but also many ways to live."

I started playing duplicate bridge with a guy who had a chronic deep cough. I finally got to know him well enough to ask what had happened to him – he was sprayed with Agent Orange in Vietnam and had pneumonia that just wouldn't go away. I said, "You're a smart guy, how did you get to Vietnam?" "My momma sent me." "What do you mean, your momma sent you?" When he was in high school, he and his buddies would get a case of beer on Friday night, put it in a cooler, go by the Holiday Inn and fill it full of ice, and then raise hell all night. One night, the manager at the Holiday Inn wrote down their license plate number, the cops stopped them, and asked where they bought the ice. He called his mother from jail and said, "Momma, I need $50 for bail money." "Son, this is a one-time thing." "Yes, ma'am." Then his mother called the Selective Service Board and said, "Draft his butt." The sergeant explained that her son was 18, hadn't graduated from high school, didn't have a job, wasn't enrolled in a college, and had a high probability of being shipped to Vietnam where there was a war going on. She said she understood all of that and repeated, "Draft his butt." So they did, he spent 2 years slogging through the jungle, survived it all, came home, and she said, "Son, I'm so glad you made it back safely." He said,

"Thank you momma." "What are you thanking me for?" "Momma, I know you called the draft board. And it was the wake-up call I needed." He finished high school, graduated from college, got an MBA at night, and spent 40 years drilling oil and gas wells all over the U.S. I'm not trying to be cute when I say that she loved her only begotten son enough to place him in harm's way to get a wake-up call through to him to save him. He has now got rid of the pneumonia through lots of antibiotics and physical therapy. His buddy that was arrested with him spent 7 days in jail.

I was teaching a 2-day seminar in Finland and felt like I was laying a giant egg. Dead silence, no questions, no comments, no discussion, no snoring, nothing. These guys didn't even need a toilet. English was not a problem as they all spoke Finnish, Swedish, and English, sometimes in the same sentence, so I was told. I spoke slowly. I spoke clearly. I repeated myself a lot. I asked if there were any questions. I asked if I needed to go back over any of the material. Nothing.

I finally staggered across the finish line (no pun intended) for lunch and asked my host, who had been there all morning, how he thought the seminar was going. He said it was probably the best seminar he had ever attended at the refinery, everyone was really enjoying it, and he was very complimentary. So I asked him why no one was saying anything. "Oh. He asked me if I knew how to find 2 Finns in a crowd of a 1000 people?" OK, we're going to play 20 questions. He said they would be standing next to each other not saying anything to each other. He was serious ! "As a people, Finns listen, we analyze, we think about what we see and hear, but we don't say anything unless we have a question." I guess that explains why there are no great Finnish humorists or stand-up comics.

My wife's stepmother married a guy named Rodney. He was her 4th husband and she owned a cemetery, but that's another story. Rodney and his 3 brothers were raised by a single mother in rural Kansas, and this story takes place about 1900. Rodney said, "We were a bunch of wild Indians, totally out of control." One day, his mother hitched the mule to the buckboard and took her 4 young boys to the nearest small town to see the local doctor, and to ask him if there was anything she could do to get them under some kind of control. The doctor examined all 4 of the boys, proclaimed them all healthy, and suggested that the oldest boy, Coleman, be given a circumcision. "Do you really think that will help?" "Yes, ma'am, I really do." "Well, when could we schedule it?" "We could do it right now back in the exam room." So without any anesthesia or painkiller, Coleman was circumcised, screaming and hollering and crying right there in the doctor's office. His mother took all 4 boys home and of course his brothers gathered around Coleman with questions. "Does it hurt?" "Oh, God, yes. Don't let the doctor do this to you !" "Can we see it?" All red and bandaged up with stitches and iodine painted all over it. "Can you still pee?" "Oh, yeah, no problem." So I said (playing the straight man), "Well, Rodney, did that calm Coleman down?" "No, but it sure calmed the other 3 of us down." I think the wise old country doctor figured 3 out of 4 was as good as he was going to do. I later met Coleman, who lived across the street from Rodney in Borger, TX and he swore it was a true story. With Rodney, you never knew.

Ralph Sharon was Tony Bennett's accompanist for over 40 years, beginning in 1957. He was given some songs written by George Cory and Douglass Cross who hoped Tony would play them. Ralph tossed them in a drawer with some shirts and forgot about them. In 1961, he was packing for a trip, saw the songs, and thought that since they were going there, he would take them along. At a hotel piano bar in Hot Springs, AR he first played "I Left My Heart in San Francisco" for Tony, who loved the song, and won his 1st 2 Grammys for it. Ralph said, "I then had to play that damned song every night for the next 40 years."

When a golfer missed the green with his approach shot, Roger Maltbie, the long-time PGA commentator said, "Well, the good news is that he's got a lot of green to work with. The bad news is that he's got a lot of green to work with." What he meant was that there was no sand or water between his ball and the hole, but he was still a long way from the hole. It depends on how you look at it.

The obituary writer for the New York Times recently retired and was asked what was the favorite obituary that she had written. Surprisingly she said it was Don Featherstone, who in 1957 sculpted the first plastic pink flamingo which forever changed suburban landscapes.

Electric cars, electric trucks, electric buses, and electric trains sound fascinating. Have any of these geniuses figured out where the electricity is coming from? We've built a huge industrial energy consumption machine in this country, businesses, cities, and homes dependent on natural gas, diesel fuel, and coal for energy. A little dab of nuclear and hydroelectric is thrown in. Solar power and wind power wouldn't even exist without the tax credits our legislatures keep giving them. And all of this infrastructure is largely hidden and taken for granted. I still remember the Senate hearing where the heads of all the major oil companies had been called to testify and one of the senators saying, "Something I've always been curious about – how do you all know to put a gas station on a street corner where there is gasoline?"

Waylon Jennings was frustrated in Nashville because he couldn't record the kind of music he wanted to make. Chet Atkins, the head of RCA Victor, had just signed Elvis Presley, a new type of talent who didn't fit any of the then recognized styles of music, and Chet had his hands full trying to figure out how to market this incredibly popular new star. So Waylon told Chet where to go, moved to Austin, and took Willie Nelson with him. And so began the *Outlaw Country* movement which created the opportunity for many more recording artists. Chet and Elvis also did all right for themselves.

A golfer was playing a course for the first time and came to a hole where he didn't know where to aim his 2nd shot. He asked his caddy who said, "Aim at the effing hotel." The golfer could see a building behind the green with the word HOTEL across the top and said to the caddy, "There's no F in hotel." The caddy shouted back at him, "Aim at the effing hotel !" A total lack of communication.

Sam and George were old friends, hadn't seen each other in a while, and bumped into each other on the street. "How are you doing, Sam?" "Oh, not too well. My knees are shot, my hips hurt, my back aches, and as you can see, I have to get around on a walker." "How are you doing, George?" "Oh, I feel like a new-born baby. I don't have a hair on my head and I think I just pissed my pants."

Jonas Blixt, a South African golfer, had just played his 1st round ever at the Masters golf tournament in Augusta, GA, and had shot a very high score. The interviewer asked him about his impressions of the course. "I loved it ! It was everything I had dreamed about and more ! It was so beautiful ! I can't wait to get out there tomorrow and play it again !" What a great attitude.

Steve Jobs: "Don't be trapped by dogma – which is living with the results of other people's thinking. Don't let the noise of others' opinions drown out your own inner voice. And most important, have the courage to follow your heart and intuition."

A friend of mine still remembers his mother taking a sheet of S&H green stamps and cutting out a rectangle that was the same shape as an inspection sticker for a car. She would then tape it on the inside left of the front windshield and they never paid to get their car inspected.

My ex-boss and I went out to play golf one day and were put with 2 other guys on the 1st tee. One of the guys was a terrible golfer and if he happened to hit the ball, he had no idea which direction it would go or how far. But he was pleasant company and told a bunch of great stories. We eventually came to a short par 3, about a 100 yards, with nothing between the tee and the green but a deep ravine with a creek at the bottom. Our erstwhile golfer breaks open a sleeve of new golf balls and my ex-boss gently suggested to him that since he hadn't been hitting it all that well today, maybe he ought to hit an old ball on this tee shot. He said, "Hell, I never have a ball long enough for it to get old."

For all you Star Trek fans, the final exam at the Starfleet Academy contained an insoluble problem, the Kobayashi Maru. It was designed to test each of the cadet's ingenuity, resourcefulness, problem solving approach, and cool-headedness under pressure, high stress but no solution. James Kirk broke into the classroom the night before, re-programmed the computer, and solved the problem the next day, the 1st cadet to ever be successful. The instructor flunked Kirk when he found out what had happened. Kirk appealed to the superintendent of the academy: "We were given a problem to solve, and I solved it. There were no stated restrictions. If I have a starship out at the edge of the solar system which develops a problem, I'm not allowed to throw up my hands and say, well, it can't be solved. I will have to solve it. My life and the lives of my crew will depend on me finding a solution." The superintendent gave Kirk a passing grade.

Tom Lehman, a long-time and very good player on the PGA tour (he has won the British Open), finally turned 50 and joined the Senior PGA Tour. When asked the difference between the 2 tours, he always tells this story: "I was playing in my 1st Seniors tournament, just walking down the fairway, when this cute young lady ducked under the ropes and started walking down the fairway beside me. She was very pretty, had a great smile, and was a very good conversationalist. I was quite flattered and enjoying her company when she asked if I was married. I said that I was, quite happily, and that we had 4 wonderful children. She said that was too bad because she had wanted to introduce me to her mother."

My wife and I were leaving on a 2 week trip to Ireland and Scotland when bad weather canceled our Dallas-London flight. After several delays, we were put on a flight to Kennedy where we would have 15 minutes to change terminals and catch a flight to London. I was carrying my wife's carry-on bag (it was heavier) and she was carrying mine. Do you see a looming problem? The sweet young thing at security decides to search my carry-on bag. She had bright red hair, a fair complexion, and looked like she was still in high school - it may have been her 1st day on the job. She opened my carry-on bag and out came cosmetics on this long table. "Are these yours?" "Yes, ma'am." Out came women's clothes. "Are these yours?" "Yes, ma'am." Out came women's shoes and underwear. "Are these yours?" "Yes, ma'am." Out came deodorant, shampoo, and hair spray. "Are these yours?" "Yes, ma'am." She called over her supervisor, showed her all the stuff spread out all over the table, and asked what she should do. Her supervisor looked at me, shrugged her shoulders, and said, "If he says it's his, let him on the plane." I must have been the 1st cross-dresser she had ever seen. I knew if I tried to explain the situation, I would never get on the plane. When I finally got to my seat, my wife asked where in the world I had been – they were holding the plane for me. I said, "You wouldn't believe it."

Stewart Cink is a long-time professional golfer on the PGA tour. He tells the story of being 17 years old and playing in a juniors tournament when he met Tiger Woods for the 1st time – Tiger was 13 years old. "He just beat the crap out of me and I could see what the next 30 years of my life were going to look like." "It was that obvious when Tiger was 13 years old?" "Oh, yeah. Everyone could see it."

Bernard Hees, CEO of Kraft Heinz: "We normally think of CEO's as the people who have the answers, right? I think CEO's are the ones who have the questions. If you can provide the right framework and questions, the consumers, clients, customers, factory managers, the supply chain – they have the answers. The important piece is to recognize and learn fast. New mistakes are welcome. But learn from the old ones. And try not to repeat the same mistakes. That means you are not learning and that is a problem in any organization. Logic gets you from point A to point B. It takes imagination to get to point C and beyond."

John Huston is a professional golfer, known for a volatile temper, who missed a 6 inch putt for a birdie. He came over to his long-time caddy and asked him for something he could break. "Why don't you try breaking par?" He was playing with John Daly and Phil Mickelson who began laughing so hard they were lying on the ground. Every time they looked at each other, they would start laughing even harder. They had to let the next group play through.

Paul Newman had a famous scene in *Butch Cassidy & the Sundance Kid* where this giant of a man with a 2 foot long knife challenges him to a knife fight. Paul walks over to him and says, "First, we have to talk about the rules for a knife fight." The giant spreads his arms out wide and says, "There ain't no rules for a knife fight!" Paul kicks him hard in a tender part of his anatomy and says, "Oh, yeah. I forgot."

Teemu Selanne is from Finland and played in the National Hockey league for 25 years for several teams. He is the only player that received a paper paycheck. He said his motivation came from looking himself in the eye in the mirror every day and knowing that he had trained hard, practiced hard, and played as hard as he could. Every 15 days he would shave, dress in a suit and tie, walk into the team's offices, and pick up his paycheck knowing he had earned every penny. How do you motivate yourself?

Clint Longley was a backup quarterback for the Dallas Cowboys. He unexpectedly replaced an injured Roger Staubach in a Thanksgiving Day game and led the Cowboys to a come-from-behind victory over the Washington Redskins. He was so unprepared and clueless that lineman Blaine Nye called it "the triumph of the uncluttered mind."

Dennis Rodman was a 6'7" professional basketball player who led the NBA in rebounding 7 years in a row, was on the all-NBA defensive team 7 times, was twice named defensive player of the year, and was inducted into the NBA Hall of Fame. One player said that having Dennis play defense against you was like wearing an extra shirt. He was famous for controversy, outlandish clothes, dyed hair, and body piercings. He would also provide "bulletin board material" for other teams by making outlandish claims about what he was going to do in a certain game or against a certain team. His coach with the Detroit Pistons, Chuck Daly, who also is in the Hall of Fame, asked him why he provoked the other players and teams: "If I don't back it up during the games, I'll be laughed at on the court, and that's not going to happen." Asked what he said back to Dennis, Chuck said, "Nothing. When in the presence of greatness, just walk away."

John McCain was a U.S. Senator from Arizona who was famous for his high energy level. He told new staff members not to worry if they find they can't keep up. "I'll still write you a very nice letter of recommendation that will get you a new job anywhere." His motto was "Don't let your coat tails hit your butt."

Mickey Gilley, Jimmy Swaggert, and Jerry Lee Lewis were cousins, all about the same age, and grew up together outside of Gramercy, LA. Jimmy's parents had a piano and Jerry Lee taught himself how to play it. Came time to graduate from high school, they were talking about what they wanted to do with their lives. Mickey Gilley said, "Well, I'm going to be a Country/Western entertainer. That's all I ever wanted to do." Jimmy Swaggert said, "I'm going to be a preacher. That's what I feel like I've been called to do." Jerry Lee Lewis was torn. Jimmy was his hero growing up, so he decided to follow him to the seminary in Waco, TX. All was going fine, until Jerry Lee decided to play *My God Is Great* boogie-woogie style in the morning assembly. The church leaders kicked him out of school, and if they had been more tolerant, Jerry Lee could have ended up being a preacher. True story, but aren't they all.

Guy Lewis was the basketball coach at the University of Houston when his secretary asked him to pay a taxi fare for a new student from Nigeria who had just arrived at his office. When the student, 7 feet tall and named Hakeem Olajuwon, had to duck his head to get into Guy's office, Guy said he instantly became a much smarter basketball coach.

I was visiting Yanbu, Saudi Arabia for the 1st time, a city on the west coast of the country on the Red Sea. I got to the Radisson Hotel late that night, but was awakened about 5AM by a loud, painful, screeching sound that seemed endless. I didn't know if it was a fire alarm, a police raid, an evacuation, or what was happening. I opened the curtains and saw a mosque right outside my window. What I had heard was the tape recording of the muezzin making the call for the 1st prayer of the day for faithful Muslims. That brings up an interesting story. The Muslims are called to prayer 5 times per day. In early times:

- The 1st prayer was supposed to be when there was enough daylight for the imam to read printed words, typically the Koran.
- The 2nd prayer was when the imam could see the sun (there are few cloudy days).
- The 3rd prayer was when a stick driven into the ground does not have a shadow (meaning the sun is directly overhead).
- The 4th prayer was when the shadow cast by the stick is as long as the stick.
- The 5th prayer of the day was when the imam could no longer read printed words.

Nowadays, it's computerized and the times are printed in the paper or listed on the internet wherever you are in the world. Also in all Muslim countries, there is an arrow on the ceiling of your hotel room pointing to Mecca.

Michael Dell was sitting in his dormitory room when his roommate asked him what was on his desk. "It's a personal computer. I'm thinking about building them." "Where?" "Right here in this room. It's just a plastic box with some electronics inside and a keyboard. How hard can it be?"

My boss and 3 other guys from the office were playing golf one day when one of them asked, "I wonder what the peasants are doing today?" My boss said, "Shhh. One of them is teeing off right now."

One of Clint Eastwood's famous quotes is from a *Dirty Harry* movie: "A man has to know his limits."

My high school basketball coach took the seniors in 1961 to see an Ohio State basketball game. Ohio State was the defending national champion, had 2 guys starting who are in the Basketball Hall of Fame (Jerry Lucas and John Havlicek) and 2 guys starting who also played pro basketball (Mel Nowell and Larry Siegfried). The 5th starter was an all-state basketball player from Ohio named Bobby Knight, who said he just threw the ball in bounds and stayed out of the way. Bobby went on to become a prolific winning college basketball coach at Indiana.

Bobby said his biggest problem as a coach was getting these high school stars, whom nobody had ever said "No" to them in their whole life, who had been pampered and protected, and then he had to get them to play defense and work together as a team. Playing the games was the easy part.

You always make the time to do something over – why not do it right the first time?

It's impossible to teach something unless you learn it first.

Bill Boeing was building furniture in his empty airplane hangar in Seattle when World War II came along and saved his airplane company.

I was leaving Presbyterian Hospital in Dallas in a wheelchair after a triple bypass operation when the attendant asked me if I minded if he asked me a question. "Of course not, what's your question?" "You've obviously been married for a long time, I'm thinking about getting married, and I was wondering if you might have some advice for me?" I'm thinking where are the Candid Cameras? I'm being wheeled out of a hospital and he wants marital advice? But I regrouped and said, "First of all, never lie to her. It never works, women are incredibly intuitive, you might be tempted to tell the 2nd lie to cover up the 1st lie, and it's a losing game. Don't go there. Second, be very careful what words you use to talk with her. If there is any possible way for your brain to disconnect from your tongue, it will happen when you least expect it, and you will have absolutely no intention of those words coming out of your mouth the way they did. Remember the story of the father counseling his son when his son started dating: You can either tell a girl that when you look at her, time stands still, or that her face would stop a clock. The words may sound similar, but your intentions and what she hears can be totally different.

My other, less fond memory of Yanbu, Saudi Arabia, was when I woke up about 2AM with a sharp pain on the lower left side of my back. I knew it was the wrong side for my appendix, so I called the front desk and asked for a doctor. Within 5 minutes, a maintenance man knocked on my door holding an adapter in his hand, what you put into a receptacle to get American electrical plugs to work. "No, no, I need a medical doctor." He scurried away. I called Tom, the American from Saudi Aramco who was traveling with me to tell him what was happening, and he said, "Oh, you've got a kidney stone." "How can you tell from your room on another floor?" "I had one last month and your symptoms sound identical." The front desk called and said I would have to pay the cab fare for a doctor and his nurse to come to the hotel. "Yes, yes, whatever, just get them here." The doctor spoke little English and the nurse none, but Tom spoke enough Arabic to get the doctor to understand my problem. I had an IV put in my arm, and the doctor stabbed the IV bag with an anti-inflammatory shot and an antibiotic. They didn't have an IV stand so there I lay on the bed in my underwear while the doctor, the nurse, the maintenance guy, and Tom took turns holding the IV bag in the air, discussing football teams and scores. It looked like a TV commercial for Sure deodorant. The next morning, I went to Yanbu General Hospital (hey, I don't have to make this stuff up) for X-rays. The X-ray technician was female, dressed in black from head to foot (all I could see were her eyes). She spoke no English, I spoke no Arabic, and we went through charades and hand signals to get me on the table to take X-rays. She wasn't allowed to touch me and we were laughing about the situation the whole time. I saw the doctor at his clinic, got 4 prescriptions, the kidney stone was gone, and I went on with my trip. The whole episode cost the equivalent of $120 and my insurance company refused reimbursement because I was out of the country.

The chief rabbi in Jerusalem called the Pope and invited him to play a round of golf with him the next time he was in Jerusalem. Of course, the Pope was very gracious and they agreed on a date and a place and said their goodbyes. The Pope turned to his monsignor and said, "I didn't want to offend the chief rabbi, but what should I do? I'm old and decrepit and have never even held a golf club in my entire life. He's old and decrepit also and can barely walk. " The monsignor suggested that they arrange a substitute to play for him. "Who is the best Catholic golfer in the world? Jack Nicklaus. "Get him on the phone." "Jack, this is the Pope – I need you to do a favor for me." "Of course, Holy Father, how may I be of service?" The Pope explained about the golf match with the chief rabbi and asked Jack to be a substitute. "I would be honored." "Let me know how the match turns out." They said their goodbyes, and a few weeks later, Jack calls back. The Pope asks how the match went. Jack says, "Holy Father, I played the best round of golf in my entire life. I hit every fairway, hit every green, and made 9 birdies in the 18 holes." "Did you win?" "No, I lost by one stroke to Rabbi Tiger Woods."

Notice that both the Pope and the chief rabbi found similar solutions to their problem.

Nolan Ryan was a major league baseball pitcher for 27 years, holds the major league record with 5,714 strikeouts, pitched 7 no-hitters, had his uniform number retired by 3 different teams, and absolutely hated to come off of the pitching mound and field a bunt. If a batter did that to him, he would get a fastball in the ribs the next time he faced Nolan.

What determines the shape of a martini glass? Its shape requires you to sip the martini slowly or you will spill the drink all over the place. You can't gulp it down. You need to know this stuff!

The chief rabbi is visiting the Pope in Rome and notices a red telephone on the desk in the Pope's private office. "What is the red telephone used for?" "Oh, my IT people installed that – it's a direct line to God – any time I need to talk to Him, I can just pick up the phone and talk to Him, any time, day or night. The chief rabbi is intrigued and asks if he can use the red phone. "Certainly." The chief rabbi finishes his call and the Pope says, "That will be $5.00 please." "Why?" "Well, that's the same rate that I pay because the IT people need to pay for the extra equipment they had to install." The chief rabbi pays.

Time goes by and the Pope is visiting the chief rabbi in Jerusalem, and notices a red telephone on the desk of the chief rabbi. "Is that what I think it is?" "Yes, I just had it installed." "Would you mind if I use it to talk to God about a few things?"

"Not at all." When the Pope finishes his conversation, the chief rabbi says, "That will be 10 cents, please." "Ten cents ! Why does it cost me $5.00 in Rome?" "Well, from here in Jerusalem, it's a local call."

I was in an office in Saudi Arabia when I noticed a poster on the wall with a picture of a lion and a gazelle standing side by side. Underneath the picture, it said:

- The lion knows that when the sun comes up, it has to run faster than the slowest gazelle, or it will starve to death.
- The gazelle knows that when the sun comes up, it has to run faster than the slowest lion, or it will be killed.
- When the sun comes up, you'd better be running.

On my first visit to Oman, my host took me to lunch in Muscat at a large super market. We stepped onto a long, shallow sloped escalator that took us up to the 1st floor (they don't count the ground floor in their numbering system). We then stepped onto a long, shallow sloped escalator that took us up to the 2nd floor. Then we walked into the Cactus Café, complete with a green neon figure of a saguaro cactus, and the worst imitation of Mexican food I have ever forced down. I know my host was trying to be nice. The interesting part of this story was when my host mentioned during lunch that money was intended to be saved, not spent. To this day, I have not figured out how or why this came into the conversation, but I have never forgotten his comment.

Charlie Pride was perhaps the first famous and successful African-American in country music. He was also the first African-American to buy a house in Highland Park, which is an expensive, exclusive, old money, incorporated city inside the city limits of Dallas, TX. He had just moved into his house and was mowing his front yard one day when this long Cadillac pulled to the curb, and the lady driving it said, "Boy, when you finish with this yard, come mow my yard." "Yes, ma'am, now which yard is that?" "It's the house on the corner, same side of this street." "Yes, ma'am, I'll get right on it." Charlie finished mowing his yard, went down the street, mowed the ladies' yard, and never heard another word from anybody.

Earl Weaver was the manager of the Baltimore Orioles professional baseball team for 17 seasons and only had one losing season. He was inducted into baseball's Hall of Fame in 1996. He was famously ejected from many games, 3 times from both games of a double header, and twice before a game had even started. He once was ejected from a game and told the umpire he was going to check the rule book. The umpire offered to let Earl use his rule book and Earl told him that he couldn't read Braille. I saw a VCR tape about Earl when he came out in the top of the 1st inning to complain to the umpire and said, "You're just out here to screw me (only he didn't use the word screw). "Yeah, Earl, that's the only reason I came to the ball park today." "All 4 of you umpires are here to screw me." "Yeah, Earl, that's just what we do." Earl then went on a 3 or 4 minute rant, calling the umpire every name he could think of, and some I had to look up. Earl never inhaled and surprisingly, the umpire did not throw Earl out of the game. The umpire finally said, "Earl, you've got a lousy baseball team. You're playing a lousy baseball team. So this is going to be a lousy baseball game. And if I have to stand here and watch it, you will too. So shut up, go sit down, and watch the game." Earl smiled, went to the dugout, and sat down.

What has caused our society to leap straight from an accusation/ allegation to punishment? The media and internet don't want to gather facts, hear testimony, have a trial, a judge or a jury, just go right to the hanging. Why is this happening? Are we so desperate to add something to the news cycle that we skip to the next shiny object lying on the beach of public opinion instead of asking whether what was said is true? Does that make us feel better about ourselves? Have we become that shallow?

Stanley Marcus was 95 years old, retired from the family store (Neiman-Marcus), doing some consulting work at home, when the phone rang. Jeff Bezos from Amazon was calling to see if Stanley would be the guest speaker at Google's next company-wide sales meeting. Stanley turned Jeff down. "I don't know anything about your business. My great-grand-daughter has just showed me how to use e-mail and turned on my 1st cell phone." "But Stanley, you know sales. You know people. You know business." Stanley eventually agreed and showed up for the sales meeting. He said, "All I could see was a sea of tee shirts." So Stanley took off his custom-made coat, his custom-made vest, his custom-made tie, his custom-made shirt, and was down to his tee shirt. "Now, we can talk." The point is how quickly Stanley knew he had to connect with his audience before they would or could listen to anything he had to say.

Our 1st neighbor here in Dallas had a cousin who flew the initial 747 Braniff flight to London. He had finished his usual pre-takeoff speech to the packed plane and thought he had turned off the microphone. He then turned to his co-pilot and said, "OK, Bob. Let's get the book out and figure out how to get this son-of-a-bitch off the ground." He said he thought every call button on the plane went off simultaneously.

Cicero: "Hindsight is the flaw of history." Read Robert Harris's 3 books of historical fiction about Cicero's life. Great story and some spooky parallels to our country.

Tony Dungy holds the career yardage record at the University of Minnesota where he played quarterback. The Pittsburgh Steelers signed him as an undrafted free agent. He is one of the few people to play in a Super Bowl (with Pittsburgh) and win a Super Bowl as a coach (the first African-American coach to do that) with Indianapolis. His teams have beaten all of the other 32 NFL teams. He is in the Pro Football Hall of Fame. His most impressive quote is that "I'm here as a servant to help all of the 53 players on my team achieve their full potential as a player. That's why I come to work every day." "What happens if in spite of your best efforts, the player just can't perform as well as he needs to for the team to be successful?" "Well, I'll get rid of him and get somebody else. We're here to win football games."

I was traveling through the Far East with a co-worker and we arrived in Tokyo in the evening and went to dinner. After dinner, we were both tired, agreed on a time for breakfast the next morning, and went to our rooms. At 1AM, my phone rings, and I'm thinking this can't be good. A voice says, "I'm back !" "John?" "Yeah, I'm back." "What do you mean, you're back?" "I decided to take a ride on the subway." "Are you all right?" "Yeah." "Where did you go?" "I don't know." "How did you get back?" "I don't know." "OK, I'll see you at breakfast." "OK." Not a word the next morning or later about his night-time tour of Tokyo. Of course, I told the story at his retirement party and embarrassed the hell out of him. We still have frequent lunches together.

An airline pilot was famous for always making perfect landings, just a touch on the runway and the plane was rolling, obviously not trained in the Navy. The chief pilot of the airline decided to take a flight with the pilot just to see how he did this, with the thought being he could then teach all the other pilots how to make perfect landings. So they take off, circle the airport, and the pilot says, "Now I just get my speed right, get my glide angle right, get my elevation right, and aim towards the end of the runway." "What do you do then?" "I wait." "What do you wait for?" "I wait for the co-pilot to scream 'Jesus Christ' and then I pull up the nose and cut the power. It's simple."

Chuck Daly, a Hall of Fame pro basketball coach, said that all of the great players (Michael Jordan, Magic Johnson, etc.) had a common trait that most spectators didn't see – a streak of meanness. That was what separated them from the other players, and it was sometimes explained away as their being super-competitive. Daly didn't agree. He says that he had stepped onto the court during a game (which is illegal) to holler some instructions to one of his players and Larry Bird went out of his way to run into him and knock him down. Daly loved it. "See what I mean?"

When Lyndon Johnson was majority leader of the U. S. Senate, he had a meeting in his office with his staff to predict the number of votes on a bill which was coming to the floor of the Senate. One of the staff members referred to one of the senators as a son-of-a-bitch. Lyndon looked over the top of his glasses and said, "He is a son-of-a-bitch, but he's our son-of-a-bitch."

Lee Trevino, a famous pro golfer, was asked when he was going to retire? "Retire to what?"

A personal story: I was taking a Finance class at SMU while getting my MBA and we had a case study to discuss that evening. I heard all these (I thought) wild and fanciful solutions to a miserable situation. The professor finally gets to me and says, "What would you do?" I said, "File Chapter 11." He said, "You get an A. You can go home now." I said, "No, I'm enjoying listening to all of these imaginative solutions." The professor said, "Just because I give you all a case study to analyze doesn't mean there is a solution to the problem."

Willie Wilson was an exceptionally fast outfielder for the Kansas City Royals. Jim Murray, one of the all-time great sportswriters, said that "Willie is so fast going from 1st base to 3rd base that none of the infielders in the league knows what he looks like."

Phil Hellmuth, a famous and very good professional poker player, is quoted as having said, "If it wasn't for luck, I would win every hand." It's a very positive, confident way of thinking.

Why is it that when something goes wacky in our country, we don't want to solve the problem, but instead immediately try to figure out who to blame? It drives me nuts.

I've dealt with jet lag for many years, and decided to start asking the stewardesses how they dealt with jet lag since they have to deal with it constantly. The results of my informal poll over several years and many flights were that they had tried all of the so-called remedies and none of them work. They said they were just goofy all the time - not a very comforting thought. A colleague did develop a way that worked for him: he forced himself to stay awake all night the day before an overseas flight – drink lots of caffeine, high sugar intake, listen to loud music, take long walks, never sit down, whatever. Then when he got on the airplane, he was so physically exhausted that he immediately slept through the whole flight. I tried it and I couldn't do it. Maybe the solution was worse than the problem.

I'm sure you have wondered about the origin of the *fist bump* seen in every type of athletic event. The story I have heard was about Moises Alou who played major league baseball from 1990-2008 and didn't wear batting gloves. He was playing for the Houston Astros and would toughen up the skin of his hands by soaking them in his own urine. His teammates refused to shake hands with him, but would touch fists, thus the origin of the fist bump. Sounds crazy enough to be true.

An enduring conclusion from my long career in the consulting business all over the world: half of the problems are technical and half are people. The technical problems can be fixed, the people problems not so easily. We've all seen people in jobs they couldn't do, people who didn't work well with others, people who couldn't take directions, it's a seemingly endless list. Think about it in your own profession.

I was on a flight from Dallas to London when the pilot announced we had mechanical problems and were diverting to Chicago where we would transfer to a spare 777, same seat assignments, and a few hours delay. Grumble, grumble. Why did American Airlines have a spare 777 sitting in Chicago? Then the pilot came back on and said not to be alarmed when we passed row 17: the passenger wasn't dead, he had taken an Ambien and was out cold. So we land in Chicago, a wheelchair is brought on board, his traveling companion made sure everything was taken off the plane, he is wheeled down through the terminal snoring away like he was snug in his bed at home, we board the second plane, and the passenger wakes up just before we get to London, not knowing anything had happened. He had a good laugh about the incident along with everyone else on board. They should put him in a commercial.

Fred Smith was getting an economics degree at Yale and had to do a term paper. He presented an idea for a package delivery company in the middle of the country to which packages would be shipped at night, separated, then delivered the next day, and promised next day delivery anywhere in the country. His professor thought the idea wasn't feasible. After 2 tours in Vietnam, he picked Memphis as the city where he started FedEx in 1973 because it had the fewest days of airport closures and was in the middle of the country. In the early days of the company, he took the last $5,000 and went to Las Vegas to play blackjack, winning $27,000, paid a $24,000 fuel bill, and kept the company alive for another week. Starting with 14 small business jets, he proved his Yale professor wrong.

Bill Parcells was the coach of the New York Giants and had a cornerback named Elvis Patterson whom he nicknamed *Toast* because he kept getting burned for touchdowns. But Bill kept playing him. When asked why, he said "Anyone can play 10 yards off the line of scrimmage, let the other team complete short passes, march down the field, and eventually score. Elvis plays up on the line, contests every pass that comes in his direction, and inevitably the other team won't convert on 3rd down, and they won't get easy scores. I'll go with *Toast* every time."

It was winter time at Chicago's O'Hare airport, bad weather, flight delays, many cancelled flights, and stranded passengers stacked up everywhere. Gate 17 was particularly over-stressed, a lone gate agent trying to cope with a flood of unhappy humanity. Into this theater of the absurd strides a pompous, self -important mogul who slams his fist on the gate agent's podium and says, "I need to be on the next flight and I want a first-class aisle seat !" The reality of the world and the current condition of the airport was obviously not worthy of his notice. The harried gate agent calmly explained such mundane items as weather delays, flight cancellations, and waiting lists that were simply beneath his consideration. He again beat his fist on the podium and said, "Do you know who I am?" The gate agent snapped, calmly turned on her microphone and said, "Attention please in the terminal. There is a gentleman here at gate 17 who doesn't know who he is. If someone in the terminal would be kind enough to come here and assist him, we would greatly appreciate it." She then left the microphone on as the irate fool told her to do something to herself that was anatomically impossible. Into the still open microphone she replied, "Sir, I'm sure there are many people in this terminal that have the same feeling that you do, but you're just going to have to get in line with everyone else." She received a standing ovation.

Ethel and Irene were 2 elderly ladies who lived next door to each other and had gotten in the habit of calling each other every morning to see if the other one was OK. One morning Irene admitted she wasn't doing well. "What's the problem?" "Well, I'm trying to work this jigsaw puzzle and it's just not making any sense." "Have you tried to find the edge pieces or the corner pieces?" "I can't find any of them." "Have you tried sorting the pieces by color?" "That doesn't work either." "What is the picture on the puzzle box?" "It's a big red rooster." "OK, I'll come over." Ethel came over to Irene's house, looked over the situation, suggested that Irene go sit in the den, and Ethel would fix her a cup of tea. Then Ethel would figure out how to get the corn flakes back in the cereal box.

Bubba Watson is from Bagdad, Florida and had always wanted to be a professional golfer. He is self-taught, started on the mini-tours, and worked his way up to the PGA tour. When he won the Masters golf tournament at Augusta in 2012, he was asked if he had ever dreamed he would win that prestigious tournament. "No, I never dreamed that big. I just wanted to make enough money to get married and have a family." He also won the Masters in 2014 and has now won a total of 14 PGA tournaments.

Robert Mondavi was a wine producer in California who wanted his sauvignon blanc wine to be different from what the other wine producers were making. So he aged it in oak barrels, where it picked up a smoky color, and he marketed it as *fume blanc*. A rose by any other name......

Great leaders set examples for their followers.

Jimmy Johnson, ex Dallas Cowboys football coach: "It's not about how many good plays you make. It's all about how many bad plays you don't make that wins football games."

I had just moved to New York City for the 2nd time in 1974 and it was summer time. Johnny Carson had endorsed a line of men's clothing and I bought 3 new suits: a non-offensive beige suit, a light blue suit, and one that had a burgundy color. I was in a packed elevator one morning headed to my office on the 22nd floor wearing my new burgundy colored suit when a friend of mine in the back of the elevator piped up and said,

"Hey, Duduit. You could jam a 2X4 up your butt and go to a masquerade party as a popsicle !" The whole elevator busted out in laughter. I also thought it was a great line and joined in the laughter. I never wore the suit again.

XVIII

CONCLUDING CHAPTER

You've now got my conclusions and observations from a long working life.

This is just a description of my journey, a way, but not the only way. You have to mark your own path in the world and my hope is that I've made it easier for you.

It's just one person's opinions, not accompanied by anyone's stamp of approval.

I think every *management* book I've ever seen was just about Biblical principles re-stated, and this book certainly is also.

I've given you a map – you have to find your own direction.

Go out and write your own book – it's called life.

May the force be with you.

Peace.

Appendix A

MY PERSONAL WORK HISTORY

- Picked peaches and bailed hay my 14th summer (2nd worst job ever)
- Two years working at a funeral home while in high school - carrying flowers, parking cars, driving cars (yes, that car), learning a lot about people, and breaking into locked churches
- Steel mill at 17 doing whatever work the union guys didn't want to do; collecting trash, picking up waste metal everywhere (blast furnace, open hearth, rolling mills, rod & wire mills, docks); recycling was a big deal; repairing and laying railroad tracks; first exposure to shift work and drinking boilermakers with breakfast.
- Co-op jobs during 5 years at college (we called it cramming 4 years of school into 5 years):
  - Draftsman at steel mill in Ohio
  - Lab technician at steel mill in Ohio
  - Statistician at steel mill in Ohio
  - Strong back and weak mind at research job in a coke plant in Kentucky (more shift work)

- Draftsman and fractionation technician at research laboratory in Ohio
- Other jobs while in college
  - Bartender on Friday and Saturday nights (learned a whole lot about people)
  - Ambulance driver (worst job ever); no schedule; just answered the phone; gory.
  - Bookstore flunkie – moved lots of books
- First job after college –19 years with a petrochemical company
  - Process engineer at two chemical plants in Texas
  - Planning/economics jobs in Houston and New York City
  - Long term planning jobs in New York City and Dallas
  - Evaluated several US coal reserves for potential new technology in a Texas plant
  - Purchased n-butane and learned natural gas liquids business in Tulsa and Houston
  - Purchased coal, visited over 50 coal mines in Colorado, Wyoming, and Montana (above and below ground), and learned a lot about railroads.
  - Purchased jet fuel and naphtha and began learning oil refining business
- Petroleum refinery consulting company – 6 years in Dallas
  - Benchmarked world-wide petroleum refinery operations
  - Benchmarked retail gasoline outlets in US
  - Supported work on bankruptcy cases

- International petroleum refining and marketing company – 2 years in Dallas and Houston
  - Lead writer for team preparing operating procedures for new refinery in Thailand
  - Wrote procedures in 6th grade level English for several operating units
  - Procedures were used to train new Thai operators unfamiliar with a refinery
- Wandered in wilderness – 2 years
  - Independent refining consultant; worked on bankruptcy cases
  - Benchmarked US retail gasoline outlets for several companies
  - Ran early morning IT center for chain of 36 liquor stores
  - Secret shopper for chain of 36 liquor stores and competitor stores
  - Analyzed performance of existing liquor stores and potential new sites
- Petroleum refinery consulting company – 19 years in Dallas
  - Benchmarked world-wide petroleum refinery operations
  - Made many cold calls all over the world looking for new clients and additional work
  - Worked in 151 refineries in 54 countries on 6 continents (Antarctica – zero)
  - Conducted over 100 two-day seminars
  - Been in 49 states; flew over Iowa lots of times
- B.S. Chemical Engineering – University of Cincinnati – 1966
- MBA – Southern Methodist University – 1980

Appendix B

SUGGESTED READING – NON FICTION

To make this list (almost all of them biographies), these books must explain history and you need to understand history to understand where we are now.

- George Washington
- John Adams
- Thomas Jefferson
- Alexander Hamilton
- Abraham Lincoln
- U. S. Grant
- Woodrow Wilson
- Theodore Roosevelt
- Franklin D. Roosevelt
- Harry Truman
- American Caesar – Douglas MacArthur – by William Manchester
- Ike – A Soldier's Story
- Omar Bradley
- George Patton
- Ronald Reagan
- George W. Bush

- Last Train to Memphis – Elvis Presley
- Charlie Daniels
- Willie Nelson
- Leonardo da Vinci
- Winston Churchill – 3 volumes by William Manchester
- Churchill – Hero of the Empire
- Tiger Woods
- Bill Parcells
- Josef Stalin – you need to understand how he came to power and the role he played in winning World War II for the Allies
- Adolf Hitler– you need to understand how he came to power and the role he played in losing World War II to the Allies
- Last Days of Night – Graham Moore
- The Nightingale's Song – Robert Timberg
- Bill O'Reilly's Killing books
- The Kingdom – Arabia and the House of Sa'ud – by Robert Lacey

Appendix C

SUGGESTED FICTION WRITERS

To make this list, whenever one of these writers put out a new book, I get a copy and read it. If you haven't read any of their books, I'm jealous of you. You're in for a treat.

- John Sandford
- Vince Flynn
- Mark Greaney
- James Lee Burke
- Harlan Coben
- Ben Coes
- Robert Ludlum
- Donna Leon
- Lisa Scottoline
- Ben Macintyre
- Sue Grafton
- John Grisham
- Jim Butcher
- James Patterson, solo
- C. J. Box
- John le Carre
- Jo Nesbo

- Ian Rankin
- Henning Mankell
- Arthur Conan Doyle
- Robert Ludlum
- Agatha Christie
- Dan Jenkins
- Nelson DeMille
- Daniel Silva
- Alex Berenson
- Ace Atkins
- Greg Iles
- Robert Parker
- Pat Conroy
- Stephen Hunter
- Jason Matthews
- Brad Meltzer
- Walter Mosley
- David Baldacci
- Robert Harris
- Randy Wayne White
- Steve Larson
- John Lescroart
- Jeffrey Deaver
- Thomas Perry
- Michael Connelly

Appendix D

REFERENCE BOOKS

- "World Order", Henry Kissinger, 2014,
- "The Blame Game", Ben Dattner, 2011, Free Press
- "Imagine", Jonah Lehrer, 2012, Houghton Mifflin Harcourt
- "Outliers", Malcolm Gladwell, 2008, Little, Brown & Co.
- "On Writing", Stephen King, 2000, Simon & Schuster
- "How We Got To Now", Steven Johnson, 2014, Riverhead Books
- "The Last Days of Night", Graham Moore
- "How We Work", Leah Weiss, 2018, Harper Collins
- "If I Understood You, Would I Have This Look On My Face?", Alan Alda, 2017, Random House
- The Bible, Old & New Testaments

Appendix E

ARTICLE FROM HARVARD BUSINESS REVIEW ON "TIME-MONKEYS"

Specifically we will deal with 3 different kinds of management time:

Boss-imposed time – to accomplish those activities which the boss requires and which the manager cannot disregard without direct and swift penalty

System-imposed time – to accommodate those requests to the manager for active support from his or her peers. This assistance must also be provided lest there be penalties, though not always direct or swift.

Self-imposed time – to do those things which the manager originates or agrees to do. A certain portion of this kind of time, however, will be taken back by subordinates and is called "***subordinate-imposed time.***" The remaining portion will be his or her own and will be called "***discretionary time.***" Self-imposed time is not subject to penalty since neither the boss nor the system can discipline the manager for not doing what they did not know the manager had intended to do in the first place.

The management of time necessitates that managers get control over the timing and content of what they do. Since what their bosses and the system impose on them are backed up by penalty, managers cannot tamper with those requirements. Thus their self-imposed time becomes their major area of concern. The managers' strategy is therefore to increase the "discretionary" component of their self-imposed time by minimizing or doing away with the "subordinate" component. They will then use the added increment to get better control over their boss-imposed and system-imposed activities. Most managers spend much more subordinate-imposed time than they even faintly realize. Hence we shall use a monkey-on-the-back analogy to examine how subordinate-imposed time comes into being and what the superior can do about it.

WHERE IS THE MONKEY?

Let us imagine that the manager is walking down the hall and that he notices one of his subordinates, Jones, coming up the hallway. When they are abreast of one another, Jones greets the manager with, "Good morning. By the way, we've got a problem. You see..." As Jones continues, the manager recognizes in this problem the same two characteristics common to all the problems his subordinates gratuitously bring to his attention. Namely, the manager knows (a) enough to get involved, but (b) not enough to make the on-the-spot decision expected of him. Eventually, the manager says, "So glad you brought this up. I'm in a rush right now. Meanwhile, let me think about it and I'll let you know." Then he and Jones part company.

Let us analyze what has just happened. Before the two of them met, on whose back was the "monkey"? The subordinate's. After they parted, on whose back was it? The manager's. Subordinate-imposed time begins the moment a monkey successfully executes a leap from the back of a subordinate to the back of his or her superior and does not end until the monkey is returned to its proper owner for care and feeding.

In accepting the monkey, the manager has voluntarily assumed a position subordinate to his subordinate. That is, he has allowed Jones to make him her subordinate by doing two things a subordinate is generally expected to do for a boss – the manager has accepted a responsibility from his subordinate, and the manager has promised her a progress report.

The subordinate, to make sure the manager does not miss this point, will later stick her head in the manager's office and cheerfully query, "How's it coming?" This is called supervision.

Or let us imagine again, in concluding a working conference with another subordinate, Johnson, the manager's parting words are, "Fine. Send me a memo on that."

Let us analyze this one. The monkey is now on the subordinate's back because the next move is his, but it is poised for a leap. Watch that monkey. Johnson dutifully writes the requested memo and drops it in his outbasket. Shortly thereafter, the manager plucks it from his inbasket and reads it. Whose move is it now? The manager's. If he does not make that move soon, he will get a follow-up memo from the subordinate (this is another form of supervision). The longer the manager delays, the more frustrated the subordinate will become (he'll be "spinning his wheels") and the more guilty the manager will feel (his backlog of subordinate-imposed time will be mounting).

Or suppose once again that at a meeting with a third subordinate, Smith, the manager agrees to provide all the necessary backing for a public relations proposal he has just asked Smith to develop. The manager's parting words to her are, "Just let me know how I can help."

Now let us analyze this. Here the monkey is initially on the subordinate's back. But for how long? Smith realizes that she cannot let the manager "know" until her proposal has the manager's approval. And from experience she also realizes that her proposal will likely be sitting in the manager's briefcase for weeks waiting for him to eventually get to it. Who's really got the monkey? Who will be checking up on whom? Wheelspinning and bottlenecking are on their way again.

A fourth subordinate, Reed, has just been transferred from another part of the company in order to launch and eventually manage a newly created business venture. The manager has said that they should get together soon to hammer out a set of objectives for the new job, and that "I will draw up an initial draft for discussion with you."

Let us analyze this one, too. The subordinate has the new job (by formal assignment) and the full responsibility (by formal delegation), but the manager has the next move. Until he makes it, he will have the monkey and the subordinate will be immobilized.

Why does it all happen? Because in each instance the manager and the subordinate assume at the outset, wittingly or unwittingly, that the matter under consideration is a joint problem. The monkey in each case begins its career astride both their backs. All it has to do now is move the wrong leg, and presto – the subordinate deftly disappears. The manager is thus left with another acquisition to his menagerie. Of course, monkeys can be trained not to move the wrong leg. But it is easier to prevent them from straddling backs in the first place.

WHO IS WORKING FOR WHOM?

To make what follows more credible, let us suppose that these same four subordinates are so thoughtful and considerate of their superior's time that they are at pains to allow no more than three monkeys to leap from each of their backs to his in any one day. In a week, the manager will have picked up 60 screaming monkeys – far too many to do anything about individually. So he spends the subordinate-imposed time juggling his "priorities."

Late Friday afternoon, a the manager is in his office with the door closed for privacy in order to contemplate the situation, while his subordinates are waiting outside to get a last chance before the weekend to remind him that he will have to "fish or cut bait." Imagine what they are saying to each other about the manager as they wait. "What a bottleneck. He just can't make up his mind. How can anyone get that high up in our company without being able to make a decision we'll never know."

Worst of all, the reason the manager cannot make any of these "next moves" is that his time is almost entirely eaten up in meeting his own boss-imposed and system-imposed requirements. To get control of these, he needs discretionary time that is in turn denied him when he is preoccupied by all these monkeys. The manager is caught in a vicious circle.

But time is a-wasting (an understatement). The manager calls his secretary on the intercom and instructs her to tell his subordinates that he will be unavailable to see them until Monday morning. At 7:00 PM, he drives home, intending with firm resolve to return tomorrow to get caught up over the weekend. He returns bright and early the next day only to see, on the nearest green of the golf course across from his office window, a foursome. Guess who?

That does it. He now knows who is really working for whom. Moreover, he now sees that if he actually accomplishes during this weekend what he came to accomplish, his subordinate's morale will go up so sharply that they will raise the limit on the number of monkeys that they will let jump from their backs to his. In short, he now sees, with the clarity of a revelation on a mountaintop, that the more he gets caught up, the more he will fall behind.

He leaves the office with the speed of a person running away from a plague. His plan? To get caught up on something else he hasn't had time for in years: a weekend with his family. This is one of the many varieties of discretionary time.

Sunday night he enjoys 10 hours of sweet, untroubled slumber, because he has clear-cut plans for Monday. He is going to get rid of his subordinate-imposed time. In exchange, he will get an equal amount of discretionary time, part of which he will spend with his subordinates to see that they learn the difficult but rewarding managerial art called, "The Care and Feeding of Monkeys."

The manager will also have plenty of discretionary time left over for getting control of the timing and content not only of his boss-imposed time but of his system-imposed time as well. All of this may take months, but compared with the way things have been, the rewards will be enormous. His ultimate objective is to manage his management time.

GETTING RID OF THE MONKEYS

The manager returns to the office Monday morning just late enough to permit his four subordinates to collect in his outer office waiting to see him about their monkeys. He calls them in, one by one. The purpose of each interview is to take a monkey, place it on the desk between them, and figure out together how the next move might conceivably be the subordinate's. For certain monkeys, this will take some doing. The subordinate's next move may be so elusive that the manager may decide – just for now - merely to sleep on the subordinate's back overnight and have him or her return with it at an appointed time the next morning to continue the joint quest for a more substantive move by the subordinate. Monkeys sleep just as soundly overnight on subordinate's backs as on superior's.

As each subordinate leaves the office, the manager is rewarded by the sight of a monkey leaving his office on the subordinate's back. For the next 24 hours, the subordinate will not be waiting for the manager; instead, the manager will be waiting on the subordinate.

Later, as if to remind himself that there is no law against his engaging in a constructive exercise in the interim, the manager strolls by the subordinate's office, sticks his head in the door, and cheerily asks, "How's it coming?" The time consumed in doing this is discretionary for the manager and boss-imposed for the subordinate.

When the subordinate (with the monkey on his or her back) and the manager meet at the appointed hour the next day, the manager explains the ground rules in words to this effect: "At no time while I am helping you with this or any other problem will your problem become my problem. The instant your problem becomes mine, you will no longer have a problem. I cannot help a person who hasn't got a problem.

"When this meeting is over, the problem will leave this office exactly the way it came in – on your back. You may ask my help at any appointed time, and we will make a joint determination of what the next move will be and which of us will make it.

"In those rare instances where the next move turns out to be mine, you and I will determine it together. I will not make any move alone."

The manager follows this same line of thought with each subordinate until at about 11:00 AM, he realizes that he has no need to shut his door. His monkeys are gone. They will return – but by appointment only. His appointment calendar will assure this.

TRANSFERRING THE INITIATIVE

What we have been driving at in this monkey-on-the-back analogy is to transfer initiative from superior to subordinate and keep it there. We have tried to highlight a truism as obvious as it is subtle. Namely before developing initiative in subordinates, the manager must see to it that they have the initiative. Once he or she takes it back, they will no longer have it and the discretionary time can be kissed goodbye. It will all revert to subordinate-imposed time.

Nor can both manager and subordinate effectively have the same initiative at the same time. The opener, "Boss, we've got a problem," implies this duality and represents, as noted earlier, a monkey astride two backs, which is a very bad way to start a monkey on its career. Let us, therefore, take a few moments to examine what we prefer to call "The Anatomy of Managerial Initiative."

There are 5 degrees of initiative that the manager can exercise in relation to the boss and to the system:

1. Wait until told – lowest initiative.
2. Ask what to do
3. Recommend, then take action
4. Act, but advise at once, or
5. Act on own, then routinely report – highest initiative

Clearly, the manager should be professional enough not to indulge in initiatives 1 and 2 in relation to either the boss or to the system. A manager who uses initiative 1 has no control over either the timing or content of boss-imposed or system-imposed time, and therefore forfeits any right to complain about what he or she is told to do or when. The manager who uses initiative 2 has control over the timing but not over the content. Initiatives 3, 4, and 5 leave the manager in control of both, with the greatest control being at level 5.

The manager's job, in relation to subordinates' initiatives, is twofold: first, to outlaw the use of initiatives 1 and 2, thus giving subordinates no choice but to learn and master "Completed Staff Work", then to see that for each problem leaving the office that there is an agreed-upon level of initiative assigned to it, in addition to the agreed-upon time and place of the next manager-subordinate conference. The latter should be duly noted on the manager's appointments calendar.

CARE & FEEDING OF MONKEYS

In order to further clarify our analogy between the monkey-on-the-back and the well-known processes of assigning and controlling, we shall refer briefly to the manager's appointments schedule, which calls for 5 hard and fast rules governing the "Care and Feeding of Monkeys" (violations of these rules will cost discretionary time):

- Rule 1 – Monkeys should be fed or shot. Otherwise, they will starve to death and the manager will waste valuable time on postmortems or attempted resurrections.
- Rule 2 – The monkey population should be kept below the maximum number the manager has time to feed. Subordinates will find time to work as many monkeys as he or she finds time to feed, but no more. It shouldn't take more than 5 to 15 minutes to feed a properly prepared monkey.
- Rule 3 – Monkeys should be fed by appointment only. The manager should not have to be hunting down starving monkeys and feeding them on a catch-as-catch-can basis.
- Rule 4 – Monkeys should be fed face-to-face or by telephone, but never by mail or e-mail.

(If by mail or e-mail, the next move will be the manager's – remember).

- Rule 5 – Every monkey should have an assigned "next feeding time" and "degree of initiative." These may be revised at any time by mutual consent, but never allowed to become vague or indefinite. Otherwise, the monkey will either starve to death or wind up on the manager's back.

CONCLUDING NOTE

"Get control over the timing and content of what you do" is appropriate advice for managing management time.

1. The **first** order of business is for the manager to enlarge his or her discretionary time by eliminating subordinate-imposed time.
2. The **second** is for the manager to use a portion of this new-found discretionary time to see to it that each subordinate possesses the initiative without which he or she cannot exercise initiative, and then to see to it that this initiative is in fact taken.
3. The **third** is for the manager to use another portion of the increased discretionary time to get and keep control of the timing and content of both boss-imposed and system-imposed time.

The result of all this is that the manager's leverage will increase, in turn enabling the value of each hour in managing management time to multiply, without theoretical limit.

Watch out for the monkeys ! The managerial woods are full of them.

Appendix F

LUCAS DAVENPORT'S BEST SONGS OF THE ROCK ERA

(as compiled by JOHN SANDFORD) – for your edification, enjoyment, & discussion. John Sandford is on my list of favorite fiction writers in Appendix C and has written 17 books with the word *Prey* in the title. Lucas Davenport is a detective in Minneapolis and is frequently listening to music when working on a case. I think my musical education stopped with Elton John, Billy Joel, the Eagles, Waylon, and Willie when I started traveling the world. I didn't know half the songs on this list. It's one person's opinion – create your own list !

"In no particular order, except that, as any intelligent person knows, any decent road trip will start with ZZ Top"

1. ZZ Top – Sharp Dressed Man
2. ZZ Top – Legs
3. Wilson Pickett – Mustang Sally
4. Crash Test Dummies – Superman's Song
5. David Essex – Rock On
6. Golden Earring –Radar Love

7. Blondie – Heart of Glass
8. Jefferson Airplane – White Rabbit
9. Jefferson Airplane – Someone To Love
10. Derek & the Dominos – Layla
11. The Doors – Roadhouse Blues
12. The Animals – House Of The Rising Sun
13. Aerosmith - Sweet Emotion
14. Aerosmith – Dude (Looks Like A Lady)
15. Bruce Springsteen – Dancing In The Dark
16. Bruce Springsteen –Born To Run
17. Bruce Springsteen – Thunder Road
18. The Police – Every Breath You Take
19. Tom Waits – Heart Of Saturday Night
20. Van Halen – Hot For Teacher
21. The Who – Who's Got Fooled Again
22. Gipsy Kings – Hotel California
23. Tracy Chapman – Give Me One Reason
24. Creedence Clearwater Revival – Down On The Corner
25. Eagles – Lyin' Eyes
26. Eagles – Life In The Fast Lane
27. Dire Straits – Skateaway (Roller Girl)
28. Tom Petty & the Heartbreakers – Mary Jane's Last Dance
29. Janis Joplin – Me And Bobby McGee
30. The Doobie Brothers – Black Water
31. Joan Jett & the Blackhearts – I Love Rock 'n' Roll
32. John Mellencamp – Jack And Diane
33. Pink Floyd – Another Brick In The Wall (Part 2)
34. Pink Floyd – Money
35. Billy Joel – Piano Man
36. Eric Clapton – After Midnight
37. Eric Clapton – Lay Down Sally
38. AC/DC – You Shook Me All Night Long

39. AC/DC – Dirty Deeds Done Dirt Cheap

40. The Hollies – Long Cool Woman (In A Black Dress)

41. Bob Dylan – Like A Rolling Stone

42. Bob Dylan – Knocking On Heaven's Door

43. Bob Dylan – Subterranean Homesick Blues

44. The Rolling Stones – (I Can't Get No) Satisfaction

45. The Rolling Stones – Brown Sugar

46. The Rolling Stones – Sympathy For The Devil

47. Sex Pistols – Anarchy In The UK

48. Grateful Dead – Sugar Magnolia

49. The Pointer Sisters – Slow Hand

50. Eurythmics – Sweet Dreams (Are Made Of This)

51. Elvis Presley – Jailhouse Rock

52. David Bowie – Ziggy Stardust

53. Bob Seger – Night Moves

54. The Everly Brothers – Bye Bye Love

55. Jimi Hendrix – Purple Haze

56. The Kinks – Lola

57. Jackson Browne – Tender Is The Night

58. The Kingsmen – Louie, Louie

59. George Thorogood & the Destroyers – Bad To The Bone

60. Metallica – Turn The Page

61. Lynryd Skynryd – Sweet Home Alabama

62. Queen – We Will Rock You

63. The Allman Brothers Band – Ramblin' Man

64. Led Zeppelin – Rock And Roll

65. Tina Turner – What's Love Got To Do With It

66. Steppenwolf – Born To Be Wild

67. U2 – With Or Without You

68. Black Sabbath – Paranoid

69. Foreigner – Blue Morning, Blue Day

70. Billy Idol - White Wedding

71. Guns N' Roses – Sweet Child Of Mine
72. Guns N' Roses – Paradise City
73. Guns N' Roses – Knockin' On Heaven's Door
74. Lou Reed – Walk On The Wild Side
75. Bad Company – Feel Like Makin' Love
76. Def Leppard – Rock Of Ages
77. Van Morrison – Brown Eyed Girl
78. Mitch Ryder & the Detroit Wheels – Devil With A Blue Dress On
79. Aretha Franklin – Respect
80. John Lee Hooker, Bonnie Raitt – I'm In The Mood
81. James Brown- I Got You (I Feel Good)
82. The Righteous Brothers – Unchained Melody
83. Prince – Little Red Corvette
84. Chuck Berry – Roll Over Beethoven
85. The Byrds – Mr. Tambourine Man
86. Crosby, Stills, Nash, & Young – Ohio
87. Buddy Holly – Peggy Sue
88. Jerry Lee Lewis – Great Balls Of Fire
89. Roy Orbison – Oh, Pretty Woman
90. Del Shannon – Runaway
91. Run-D.M.C.- Walk This Way
92. Otis Redding – (Sittin' On) The Dock Of The Bay
93. Nirvana – Smells Like Teen Spirit
94. Paul Simon – Still Crazy After All These Years
95. Bo Diddley – Who Do You Love?
96. Brewer & Shipley – One Toke Over The Line
97. Ramones – I Wanna Be Sedated
98. The Clash – Should I Stay Or Should I Go
99. Talking Heads – Burning Down The House
100. Dmitri Shostakovich – Jazz Suite No. 2: Waltz 2

Appendix G

THE PURSUIT OF HAPPINESS

"What if, as a caged white rat learns to press a lever in order to get food, we could learn to press our own mental buttons and voila: happiness? Could we train ourselves so well that we'd start to get happy in anticipation, a la Pavlov's dog with food?

The short answers: we can, and yes.

Of course, the truth is way complicated. The study of happiness reaches back thousands of years, to philosophers you've (probably) never heard of. It deals with the human brain, still a mystery even to neurologists. And these days, it's making its way through academic journals and conferences and university classrooms, bubbling up into the popular press every once in a while, like now. Happiness – just what is it? What causes it? Can it be cultivated?

The answers to these questions, once the province of philosophy, now belonging to positive psychology, a newish branch of the psychology profession that studies healthy ninds rather than sick ones, Thanks to positive psychologists, we now know the following:

1. The things we think will make us happy often don't.
2. Money does not make us happy.
3. Having more money than our neighbors might.
4. And having less than the neighbors is guaranteed to interfere, big-time.
5. Friends and family do make us happy.
6. Moving away from them for a new job doesn't.
7. Old fogies are happier than the young.
8. Beautiful people aren't happier than the rest of us, they just look better unhappy.
9. Having lots of choices doesn't make us happy; it seriously stresses us out.
10. Oh, and commuting is an immense drag on gross national happiness.

Also, thanks to positive psychology, we now know that a big chunk of our individual happiness is genetic. We have a natural set point – a sort of happiness zone - that we're stuck with. So if we're not naturally cheery, no amount of therapy will make us so (thanks, Mom and Dad). But there are flavors of happiness we can control, or, in the language of the Declaration of Independence, pursue.

In fact, we can even take courses in how to craft such a pursuit. The godfather of positive psychology, Martin Seligman, PHD, director of the University of Pennsylvania's Positive Psychology Center, launched the first such course in 2003. Before long, universities across the United States – including the University of California, Berkeley, Princeton, and the University of Texas – added similar courses to their curricula. Tal Ben-Shear's positive-psychology class is the single most popular course at Harvard University.

The syllabi for these classes should carry this black-box warning, if not about the courses themselves, then about chasing felicity in general: It's hard work. As Benjamin Franklin observed, the Declaration of Independence only gives people the right to pursue happiness, you have to catch it for yourself.

HAPPINESS IS:

- A good habit
- A butterfly that will rest on your shoulder if you are still enough
- A cudgel optimists use to beat pessimists silly

Positive psychology as a discipline wants to set in motion a positive-feedback loop: Think good thoughts and you'll be happy, do good and you'll feel good, smile and the world smiles with you, etc. The happier you are, the more good thoughts you'll have. And the more good things you do, the happier you'll become.

Of course, the details of each approach are more nuanced, but in essence, this is the philosophy: Negative leads to negative, and positive leads to positive.

The thing is, some people think good thoughts naturally. Other people – and not just the Eeyore types – have to be tricked into it. Lead them to tiptoe through the tulips repeatedly and regularly, preferably taking a few detours to do good and be nice, and said tiptoeing becomes habitual for them. Habitual positive thinking equals habitual happiness.

At least, theoretically.

Just as physical exercise is proven to stave off heart disease and cancer, happiness exercise is shown, in study after study, to actually aid emotional resilience. But although well-meaning doctors, medical researchers, and government types have pounded the physical exercise drum for decades, people aren't exactly thronging the gym or track. Happiness calisthenics, which are still new and not widely publicized, have even fewer adherents. As anyone who's ever tried to keep a New Year's resolution knows, we mortals resist change about as much as we resist paying taxes. If sticking to good habits were a cinch, everyone you know would be fit and healthy, have a clean desk, a lint-free dryer filter, and absolutely no credit card debt.

These techniques are guaranteed to boost your happiness quotient – and not just momentarily:

- <u>Three a day for better health</u> – This is an exercise for your gratitude muscle. Every night, write down 3 things you were thankful for that day. The key phrase is *every night*.
- <u>Play to your strengths</u> – Identify your character strengths – curiosity, perseverance, self-control, etc. Even better, apply them to a task you detest. (Go to <u>www.authentichappiness.org</u> and take the VIA Signature Strengths Questionnaire.)
- <u>Get in the flow</u> – Take on a challenge that's barely within your grasp. The act of stretching to do something difficult – but not beyond you – will get you into that blissful state called flow, when time tends to stop and the world seems to disappear. Do it regularly. You'll be happier even when you're not flowing. (For more on flow, start with Mihaly Csikszentmihalyi. It's an tire branch of very interesting research.)

- <u>Serve somebody</u> – Volunteer. Helping other people will make you happier for as long as you keep doing it.

You can lead a human to the happiness well, it appears, but getting them to come drink every day is another story.

HAPPINESS IS:

- A perfect score on a positive-psychology quiz.
- A point of view that can be taught.
- Like intelligence – you either have it or you don't. But with education, good actors can fake it well enough to fool a Freudian.

We can indoctrinate the young by teaching happiness in school – something that is already happening. Perhaps the strangest thing about these classes isn't the fact that they exist or that they're immensely popular but what happens after the semester is finished and the syllabus is filed away.

"Some students got really excited, sent me letters later, the kind of letters I've never received before," says Mark Setton, a University of Bridgeport philosophy professor who teaches a course that explores psychological perspectives on happiness. "One student was going to commit suicide and stopped herself by concentrating on something I'd taught during that course. I realized this stuff can change people.

In true trickle-down fashion, the teaching of positive-psychology techniques is spreading to high schools and even some elementary schools. Setton is one of the people trying to get it to trickle faster. He started the website pursuit-of-happiness.org as a go-to portal for teachers who want a little happiness in their classrooms. Eventually, he'd like to have an entire happiness curriculum, every lesson a multimedia wonder, in order to get the happiness gospel to as many people as possible. When we talked, he'd just received an e-mail from a potential happiness teacher in Nepal.

Amy Fineburg, a high school teacher in Alabama, teaches a positive –psychology unit and helped develop an American Psychological Association curriculum for secondary students. It's free to anyone who requests it. Her own students are eager consumers. "Intuitively it's something they want to know about," she says.

These classes include some of the new happiness theory as well as practical exercises to put the theory to the test. Almost all of them require what's known in positive - psychology parlance as a "gratitude visit" or a "gratitude letter." It involves writing a thank-you note - to a former teacher, a grandparent, a coach, or anyone you haven't properly thanked for something – and presenting it to the recipient in person. The act of writing (and delivering) that letter single-handedly makes the sender happier. And studies show the effects last for a full month.

Easy, right? So easy a child could do it? Well, not necessarily. Children might be able to do it, but the effect might not be as pronounced as it is in adults who've been harboring overdue thank-yous for years. Researchers have actually tested one positive-psychology exercise on kids and adults. It did a bang-up job on the grownups but affected the kids more like a whimper. The truth is, positive psychology is so new, there hasn't been time for multiyear studies of children who've learned the drill versus those who've never heard of it. Common sense says that focusing on older kids is probably the best bet.

"My gut feeling is that you can teach a few specific techniques to kids in junior high but that in general, kids would be much more able to profit from these lessons beginning around age 16 or 17," says Jonathan Haidt, a University of Virginia professor whose specialty is studying morality, and its relationship to happiness.

Haidt wrote *"The Happiness Hypothesis: Finding Modern Truth in Ancient Wisdom"*, which while optimistic that the rapidly unfolding knowledge about happiness can help people, is pointedly skeptical of overnight success. The danger of positive psychology is that the exercises are simple – not simplistic – but in a Thoreauvian kind of way. Did you like that word? Like many difficult things in life, they sound easy. And Haidt makes the point that sounding easy and being easy are as far apart as Los Angeles and Cairo. The human mind is a mysterious thing, the product of thousands of years of evolution, a marriage of hunter-gatherer spear-carrying man and contemporary iPod/cell phone man. We're not entirely in control of our own impulses. Yet by dint of hard work and much gratitude, you, too, can be happier. It's just not as instant as potato flakes. **HAPPINESS IS A CHOICE!**

ACKNOWLEDGEMENTS

Other inspirers to whom I owe thanks, in no particular order, are: Bill Coriell, the Dodson brothers, Harold Duduit, Ed Duduit, Art Duvendeck, Jaime de Sostoa, J. C. Duvall, E.W. Eckey, Jack Shipley, Ron Santilli, Max Webb, Huey Prater, Gene Steel, Blanchard Pritchard, John Lauer, Homer Wilson, Emil Tejml, Phil Turek, Don Merino, Jim Stewart, Paul Liscom, Ron Vandenberg, Larry James, Coy Hood, Jack Cockburn, Lee Solomon, David Capers, Ken Hornik, Bill Westfall, Kevin Gormley, Bob Honeycutt, David Bossung, the Trouts, John Wise, the Zeiglers, the Knollins, Shirley Poska, the Lamptons, the Essons, Waynel Sexton, the Kilisheks, and countless clients from 54 countries all over the world.

I would never have achieved anything without the kind advice and support I received from all of the above people. I have been blessed.

I had clients in Russia who traveled with me all over their country. Every year when they visit Dallas, they still take Pat and I out to dinner. I could not ask for any greater affirmation.

inted in the United States
Bookmasters